2ND EDITION

Wildflowers
of Arizona
Field Guide

Nora Mays Bowers,
Rick Bowers,
and Stan Tekiela

PUBLICATIONS
Adventure
an imprint of AdventureKEEN

Dedication

To my sister, Beth, for sharing her love of flowers with me —Nora

To Matt Johnson, who always kept plants on my mind and taught me so much about them —Rick

To my daughter, Abigail Rose, the sweetest flower in my life —Stan

Edited by Deborah Walsh

Proofread by Emily Beaumont

Cover, book, and icon design by Jonathan Norberg

PHOTO CREDITS

All photos are copyright by **Rick and Nora Bowers** unless otherwise noted.
Cover photo: Desert Mariposa Lily by **Rick Bowers**

P. J. Alexander: 270; **James M. Andre:** 278 (fruit); **Ralph Arvesen:** 130; **Larry Blakely:** 118; **Kenneth L. Bowles:** 288; **Michael L. Charters:** 190 (inset), 421 (Sow-thistle); **Christopher L. Christie:** 266 (dried stems), 308 (inset), 308 (main), 394; **Dudley Edmondson:** 8 (spike left, round right, flat both), 9 (bell right, irregular left, tube left), 10 (twice compound both, palmate left), 11 (alternate both), 254; **Thomas J. Elpel:** 104; **Richard Haug:** 144; **Dick Henderson/www.saguaro-juniper.com:** 240; **Steven Katovich/Bugwood.org:** 412 (main); **T Beth Kinsey:** 88 (both), 242 (fruit), 258 (main), 292, 384; **Tom Koerner/U.S. Fish and Wildlife Service:** 106 (fruit); **Thomas Kornack:** 364 (main); **Lara Hartley Photography:** 166; **Glen Lee:** 228; **Don Mammoser:** 218 (fruit), 344, 420 (alfalfa); **Craig Martin /iNaturalist.org:** 330 (inset); **Gary A. Monroe/USDA-NRCS Plants Database:** 190 (main), 204, 216; **Randy Morse/Golden State Images:** 266 (main); **Steve Mortenson:** 9 (regular left), 12; **Robert Potts /California Academy of Sciences:** 154; **Rob Routledge/Sault College/Bugwood.org:** 330 (main); **Larry Sansone:** 166; **Alan Schmierer/flickr.com:** 408 (inset); **Al Schneider:** 136, 262, 278 (main); **Stan Tekiela:** 8 (round left), 9 (irregular right, tube right), 10 (compound left, palmate right, simple right, simple lobed both), 18 (both), 30, 32, 62 (fruit), 72, 90, 96, 128 (both), 160, 162, 188, 196, 214, 218 (main), 256, 272, 282 (both), 346, 388, 404 (fruit), 408 (main), 420 (Bindweed), 420 (Dandelion & Mullein), 421 (Clover, Morning Glory, Shepherd's Purse); **Andy and Sally Wasowski:** 208; **Kay Yatskievych:** 222; and **Gena Zolotar:** 86 (main).

Images used under license from Shutterstock.com:
Vahan Abrahamyan: 346 (inset); **chyworks:** 432; **Dominic Gentilcore PhD:** 114; **Laurens Hoddenbagh:** 172; **Daniel Koglin:** 278 (flower); **Sarah Scott:** 86 (inset); and **Sean Xu:** 56.

10 9 8 7 6 5 4 3 2 1

Wildflowers of Arizona Field Guide
First Edition 2008, Second Edition 2024
Copyright © 2008 and 2024 by Nora Mays Bowers, Rick Bowers, and Stan Tekiela
Published by Adventure Publications, an imprint of AdventureKEEN
310 Garfield Street South
Cambridge, Minnesota 55008
(800) 678–7006
www.adventurepublications.net
All rights reserved
Printed in China
Cataloging-in-Publication data is available from the Library of Congress
ISBN 978-1-64755-395-1 (pbk.); 978-1-64755-396-8 (ebook)

TABLE OF CONTENTS

ARIZONA AND WILDFLOWERS

Arizona is a great place for wildflower enthusiasts! From high mountains with cool pine forests and refreshing streams to the driest and hottest deserts, Arizona is home to a unique variety of wonderful wildflowers.

In this edition, we have omitted cacti, as our *Cacti of Arizona* is now available. For common invasive or nonnative species, see page 420. These changes allowed us to include more indigenous flowers—200 species in all. That is important because we are losing many native species to human development and agriculture. Native bees and other wildlife evolved alongside the native plants and generally cannot utilize the introduced plants for food or reproduction. You can help by planting native plants for the preservation of our wildlife, hummingbirds, bees, and butterflies. So when landscaping, we encourage you to ensure that your plants are indigenous to your state and placed at the elevation at which they naturally occur. Don't spray with pesticides, as the caterpillars and larvae you allow to live will feed the wild birds or turn into attractive butterflies and moths.

STRATEGIES FOR IDENTIFYING WILDFLOWERS

Determining the color of the flower is the first step in a simple five-step process to identify a wildflower.

Because this field guide is organized by color, identifying an unknown wildflower is as simple as matching the color of the flower to the color section of the book. The color tabs on each page identify the color section.

The second step in determining the identity of a wildflower is to note the size. Within each color section, the flowers are arranged by the size of the flower, or flower cluster, from small to large. A plant with a single, small yellow flower will be in the beginning of the yellow section, while a large white flower will be towards the end of the white section. Sometimes flowers are made up of many individual flowers in clusters that are perceived to be one larger flower. Therefore, these will be ordered by the size of the cluster, not the individual flower. See page 432 for rulers to help estimate flower and leaf size.

Once you have determined the color and approximate size, observe the appearance of the flower. Is it a single flower or cluster of flowers? If it is a cluster, is the general shape of the cluster flat, round, or spike? For the single flowers, note if the flower has a regular, irregular, bell, or tube shape. Also, counting the number of petals might help to identify these individual flowers. Compare your findings with the descriptions on each page. Examining the flower as described above should result in narrowing the identity of the wildflower down to just a few candidates.

The fourth step is to look at the leaves. There are several possible shapes or types of leaves. Simple leaves have only one leaf blade but can be lobed. Compound leaves have a long central leaf stalk with many smaller leaflets attached. Twice compound leaves have two or more leaf stalks and many leaflets. Sometimes it is helpful to note if the leaves have toothed or smooth margins (edges), so look for this also.

For the fifth step, check to see how the leaf is attached to the stem. Some plants may look similar but have different leaf attachments, so this can be very helpful. Look to see if the leaves are attached opposite of each other along the stem, alternately, or whorled around a point on the stem. Sometimes the leaves occur at the base of the plant (basal). Some leaves do not have a leaf stalk and clasp the stem at their base (clasping), and in some cases the stem appears to pass through the base of the leaf (perfoliate).

Using these five steps (color, size, shape, leaves, and leaf attachment) will help you gather the clues needed to quickly and easily identify the common wildflowers of Arizona.

USING THE ICONS

Sometimes the botanical terms for leaf type, attachment, and type of flower can be confusing and difficult to remember. Because of this, we have included icons at the bottom of each page. They can be used to quickly and visually match the main features of the plant to the specimen you are viewing, even if you don't completely understand the botanical terms. By using the photos, text descriptions, and icons in this field guide, you should be able to quickly and easily identify most of the common wildflowers of Arizona.

The icons are arranged from left to right in the following order: flower cluster type, flower type, leaf type, leaf attachment, and fruit. The first two flower icons refer to cluster type and flower type. While these are not botanically separate categories, we have made separate icons for them to simplify identification.

Flower Cluster Icons

    (icon color is dependent on flower color)

Flat   Round   Spike

Any cluster (tightly formed group) of flowers can be categorized into one of three cluster types based on its overall shape. The flat, round, and spike types refer to the cluster shape, which is easy to observe. Technically there is another cluster type, composite, which appears as a single daisy-like flower but is actually a cluster of many tiny flowers. Because this is often perceived as a flower type, we have included the icon in the flower type section. See page 9 for its description.

Some examples of cluster types

Flat   **Round**   **Spike**

Flower Type Icons

(icon color is dependent on flower color)

Regular   Irregular   Bell   Tube   Composite

Botanically speaking, there are many types of flowers, but in this guide, we are simplifying them to five basic types. Regular flowers are defined as having a round shape with three or more petals, lacking a disk-like center. Irregular flowers are not round but uniquely shaped with fused petals. Bell flowers are hanging with fused petals. Tube flowers are longer and narrower than bell flowers and point up. Composite flowers (technically a flower cluster) are usually round compact clusters of tiny flowers appearing as one larger flower.

Some examples of flower types

Regular   Irregular   Bell

Tube   Composite   disk flowers   ray flowers

Composite cluster: Although a composite flower is technically a type of flower cluster, we are including the icon in the flower type category because most people who are unfamiliar with botany would visually see it as a flower type, not a flower cluster. A composite flower consists of petals (ray flowers) and/or a round disk-like center (disk flowers). Sometimes a flower has only ray flowers, sometimes only disk flowers or both.

Leaf Type Icons

| Simple | Simple Lobed | Compound | Twice Compound | Palmate |

Leaf type can be broken down into two main types: simple and compound. Simple leaves are leaves that are in one piece; the leaf is not divided into smaller leaflets. It can have teeth or be smooth along the edges. The simple leaf is depicted by the simple leaf icon. Simple leaves may have lobes and sinuses that give the leaf a unique shape. These simple leaves with lobes are depicted by the simple lobed icon.

Some examples of leaf types

Simple   **Simple Lobed**   **Compound**

Twice Compound   **Palmate**

Compound leaves have two or more distinct, small leaves called leaflets that arise from a single stalk. In this field guide we are dividing compound leaves into regular compound, twice compound, or palmately compound leaves. Twice compound leaves are those that have many distinct leaflets arising from a secondary leaf stalk. Palmately compound leaves are those with three or more leaflets arising from a common central point.

Leaf Attachment Icons

Alternate   Opposite   Whorl   Clasping   Perfoliate   Basal

Leaves attach to the stems in different ways. There are six main types of attachment, but a plant can have two different types of attachments. This is most often seen in the combination of basal leaves and leaves that attach along the main stem either alternate or opposite (cauline leaves). These wildflowers have some leaves at the base of the plant, usually in a rosette pattern, and some leaves along the stem. In these cases, both icons are included; for most plants, there will only be one leaf attachment icon.

Some examples of leaf attachment

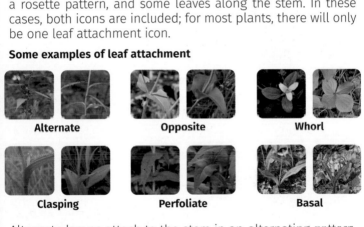

Alternate   Opposite   Whorl

Clasping   Perfoliate   Basal

Alternate leaves attach to the stem in an alternating pattern, while opposite leaves attach to the stem directly opposite from each other. Whorled leaves have three or more leaves that attach around the stem at the same point. Clasping leaves have no stalk, and the base of the leaf partly surrounds the main stem. Perfoliate leaves are also stalkless and have a leaf base that completely surrounds the main stem. Basal leaves are those that originate at the base of a plant, near the ground, usually grouped in a round rosette.

Fruit Icons

  (icon color is dependent on berry or pod color)

Berry **Pod**

In some flower descriptions a fruit category has been included. This may be especially useful when a plant is not in bloom or when the fruit is particularly large or otherwise noteworthy. Botanically speaking, there are many types of fruit. We have simplified these often-confusing fruit categories into two general groups, berry and pod.

Some examples of fruit types

Berry **Pod**

The berry icon is used to depict a soft, fleshy, often-round structure containing seeds. The pod icon is used to represent a dry structure that, when mature, splits open to release seeds.

BLOOMING SEASON

Most wildflowers have a specific season of blooming. You probably won't see, for example, the spring-blooming desert mariposa lily blooming in summer or fall. In the lower deserts of Arizona, spring (February) and summer (beginning of May) come earlier—and fall (late October) comes later—than it does in the higher mountains and in most of the rest of the United States, so we have specified the months, rather than the seasons, during which a wildflower blooms. Knowing the months of bloom can help you narrow your selection as you try to identify an unknown flower.

LIFE CYCLE/ORIGIN

The life cycle of a wildflower describes how long a wildflower lives. Annual wildflowers are short-lived. They sprout, grow, and bloom in only one season, never to return except from seed. Most wildflowers have perennial life cycles that last many years. Perennial wildflowers are usually deeply rooted plants that grow from the roots each year. They return each year from their roots, but they also produce seeds to start other perennial plants. Similar to the annual life cycle is the biennial life cycle. This group of plants takes two seasons of growth to bloom. In the first year, the plant produces a low growth of basal leaves. During the second year, the plant sends up a flower stalk from which it produces seeds for starting new plants. However, the original plant will not return for a third year of growth.

Origin indicates whether the plants are native or nonnative. All of the wildflowers in this book are native to Arizona. Nonnative plants are frequently introduced unintentionally when they escape from gardens and farms. These introduced plants often become invasive, harming the ecosystems of the natural habitat.

LIFE ZONES/HABITATS

Sometimes noting the habitat surrounding a flower in question can be a clue to its identity. In Arizona, ecologists define nine distinct life zones, but for simplicity in this book, only seven will be considered. These life zones have characteristic plant and animal species based on temperature differences found at various elevations combined with yearly rainfall. The elevation range of a life zone is related to how far north or south in Arizona the zone occurs and how much rain the zone receives, thus the elevational ranges may overlap. Some plants are only found in certain life zones; others are generalists and can be found in more than one zone or even in all seven.

Desert scrub habitats range 100–6,500 feet (30–1,980 m), but more importantly, this life zone is defined by rainfall of 12 inches (30 cm) or less per year. The dominant variety of shrubs of this zone is dependent upon the zone's location in Arizona and the type of desert in which the zone occurs. It is unique due to the presence of a wide variety of cacti, from the giant saguaro, which can be as tall as a power pole, to tiny pin-cushion cacti. Some of the wildflowers in this book, such as California poppy, arroyo lupine, or owl's clover, are short-lived annuals (ephemerals) that only grow and bloom in the deserts after good winter rains.

At some elevations, the **grasslands** life zone mixes with or replaces desert scrub habitats. Grasslands range 3,000–7,000 feet (915–2,135 m) and have rainfall averages of 17 inches (43 cm) or less per year. Pure grasslands contain mostly shrubless stands of grasses, with some scattered evergreen oaks and mesquite trees. This zone suffers from overgrazing by cattle and the introduction of exotic grasses. New Mexico thistles are common along roads in this life zone during spring, and summer poppies bloom over large areas following the summer rains.

Running roughly east to west in a broken band just south of the rim of the Grand Canyon lies the **interior chaparral** life zone. It ranges 3,000–8,000 feet (915–2,440 m) and has an annual rainfall of 15–25 inches (38–64 cm). Interior chaparral consists of a unique, dense community of deep-rooted evergreen shrubs and trees that have adapted to a habitat defined by frequent fires and that can easily regrow following fire. Palmer penstemons, blackfoot daisies, and dogweed are typical wildflowers found in this life zone.

Oak/pinyon pine/juniper woodlands occur at elevations between 4,000–7,000 feet (1,220–2,135 m) with yearly rainfall averaging 12–24 inches (30–61 cm). Sometimes this habitat overlaps with the grasslands, with grasses growing beneath widely spaced trees. In northern Arizona, this zone includes several species of evergreen juniper trees, as well as pinyon pines. Evergreen oaks mixed with pinyon pines are predominant in this zone in southern Arizona, where the bright lavender wildflower, Dakota mock vervain, is often found growing beneath oaks.

The **riparian deciduous** life zone lies within all the other life zones, but only near streams or dry streambeds with intermittently running surface water (washes). In soils around dry washes, underground streams supplement the moisture supplied by sporadic rain or snow, providing water to deep-rooted plants. Columbines, larkspurs and monkeyflowers are some of the wildflowers commonly found in riparian soils. However, moisture-loving, usually riparian plants can be found far from streams at higher and cooler elevations, where more rain falls and evaporative water loss is reduced. During drought, desert-adapted wildflower species, such as lupines and fleabane, also concentrate near streams and washes. Most plants seen in areas around streams are larger than usual due to the increased moisture in the soil. "Riparian," from the Latin **riparus**, means "bank" and refers to the land adjoining streams, while "deciduous" applies to the many tree species in this zone that shed their leaves in autumn.

With a range of 6,000–9,000 feet (1,830–2,745 m) and 20–30 inches (50–76 cm) of annual rainfall, the **montane** life zone contains open, park-like, coniferous forests dominated by ponderosa pines. On cooler and moister north-facing slopes, fir trees may mix with the pines. Other species in this zone include evergreen oaks as well as deciduous maples and aspens. Forest meadows and understories (the shady habitats beneath forest canopies) provide a rich environment for many wildflowers, including blue bonnet lupines and pineywoods geraniums.

The **subalpine** life zone, at 8,000–11,500 feet (2,440–3,510 m), receives 30–45 inches (76–114 cm) of annual precipitation, coming mostly in the form of snow. It is densely forested with the trees shading the forest floor more than they do in the montane zone. Thus, there are few plants that grow under the trees (understory). Coniferous trees such as spruces, firs and pines, and broad-leaf aspens are dominant here. Water is abundant, giving rise to lush meadows and carpets of wildflowers in forest openings (where sunlight is available). Canada violets and cardinalflowers are common in these cool, moist forests.

RANGE

The wide variety of life zones in Arizona naturally restricts the range of certain wildflowers that have specific requirements. Sometimes this section can help you eliminate a wildflower from consideration based solely on its range. However, please keep in mind that the ranges indicate where the flower is most commonly found. They are general guidelines only and there will certainly be exceptions to these ranges.

NOTES

The Notes are sometimes fun and fact-filled with many gee-whiz tidbits of interesting information such as historical uses, other common names, insect relationship, color variations, and much more. Much of the information in this section cannot be found in other wildflower field guides.

CAUTION

In the Notes, it is mentioned that in some cultures, some of the wildflowers were used for medicine or food. While some find this interesting, DO NOT use this guide to identify edible or medicinal plants. Some of the wildflowers in Arizona are toxic or have toxic look-alikes that can cause severe problems. Do not take the chance of making a mistake. Please enjoy the wildflowers with your eyes or camera. In addition, please don't pick, trample, or transplant any wildflowers you see. The flower of a plant is its reproductive structure; if you pick a flower, you have eliminated its ability to reproduce. Transplanting wild-flowers is another destructive occurrence. Most wildflowers need specific soil types, pH levels, or special bacteria or fungi in the soil to grow properly. If you attempt to transplant a wild-flower to a habitat that is not suitable for its particular needs, the wildflower most likely will die. Also, some wildflowers, due to their dwindling populations, are protected by laws that forbid you to disturb them. Many Arizona wildflowers are now available at local garden centers. These wildflowers have been cultivated and have not been dug from the wild.

Enjoy the wild wildflowers!

Nora, Rick, and Stan

leaves

Common Name
Scientific name

Color Indicator —

Family: plant family name

Height: average range of mature plant

Flower: general description, type of flower, size of flower, number of petals

Leaf: general description, size, leaf type, type of attachment, toothed or smooth

Fruit: berry or pod

Bloom: spring, summer, fall

Cycle/Origin: annual, perennial, biennial, native, nonnative

Zone/Habitat: zones such as desert scrub, grasslands, interior chaparral, oak/pinyon pine/juniper woodlands, riparian deciduous, montane or subalpine and elevation ranges; places found, may include soil types

Range: an approximate range where the flower is found

Stan's Notes: helpful identification information, history, origin, and other interesting, "gee-whiz" nature facts

Not all icons are found on every page. See preceding pages for icon descriptions.

CLUSTER TYPE
Spike

FLOWER TYPE
Tube

LEAF TYPE
Simple

LEAF ATTACHMENT
Opposite

LEAF ATTACHMENT
Perfoliate

FRUIT
Pod

Miniature Woolly Star
Eriastrum diffusum

Family: Phlox (Polemoniaceae)

Height: 1–8" (2.5–20 cm)

Flower: tubular star-shaped flower, ½" (1 cm) wide, is blue to lavender to whitish, has 5 fused petals spreading into pointed lobes around a yellow center; held by 5 woolly, whitish-green sepals; loosely grouped flowers are backed by woolly, dark-green bracts

Leaf: narrowly lance-shaped leaves, ½–1" (1–2.5 cm) long, are smooth or woolly above with smooth or lobed margins; fluffy wool at leaf attachments (axis); white-haired, reddish-brown stems

Bloom: Mar–Jun

Cycle/Origin: annual; native

Zone/Habitat: desert scrub and grasslands at 1,000–5,000' (305–1,525 m); flats, along washes, playas, mesas

Range: throughout

Notes: The genus name *Eriastrum* is from the Greek word *erion* for "wool" and *astrum* for "star," meaning that the plants are "woolly with star-like flowers." After heavy winter rains, this beautiful little flower can carpet large areas of deserts in Arizona. The seeds can be purchased from nurseries for cultivation. The only other *Eriastrum* in Arizona, the very similar desert woolly star (*E. eremicum*) (not shown), occurs in the western two-thirds of Arizona; has slightly larger flowers with 2–6 lobes; and has fewer, narrower leaves.

FLOWER TYPE   LEAF TYPE   LEAF ATTACHMENT
Tube   **Simple**   **Alternate**

Franciscan Bluebells
Mertensia franciscana

Family: Forget-me-not (Boraginaceae)

Height: 12–36" (30–91 cm)

Flower: groups of drooping, light- to dark-blue flowers; each slender bell-shaped flower, ⅝" (1.5 cm) long, has 5 rounded lobes; can be purplish blue to pink or white

Leaf: lance-shaped, dark-green leaves, 1–5" (2.5–13 cm) long, fuzzy above with prominent veins and pointed tips; alternate, but pairs of leaves at the end of stems are opposite; leaves turn red or purple in autumn

Bloom: Jun–Sep

Cycle/Origin: perennial; native

Zone/Habitat: montane and subalpine at 6,000–11,500' (1,830–3,510 m); under ponderosa pines or fir trees, along streams

Range: northeastern and southeastern corners of Arizona

Notes: This tall plant is common along streams, in moist meadows, and in forest clearings. It grows as a single plant, in small groups, or in large dense colonies with hundreds of blooms. Franciscan bluebells can be found on the San Francisco Peaks, the tallest mountains in Arizona. These peaks ring a dormant volcano and are sacred to Navajo, Hopi, and Havasupai Peoples. The species name *franciscana* is for these mountains, which Europeans named in honor of the Catholic saint, St. Francis.

FLOWER TYPE **Bell**   LEAF TYPE **Simple**   LEAF ATTACHMENT **Alternate**

Arizona Morning Glory
Evolvulus arizonicus

Family: Morning Glory (Convolvulaceae)

Height: 1–4' (30–122 cm)

Flower: flat, round flower of sky blue to purplish blue (sometimes white), ¾" (2 cm) wide, has 10 fused petals and sepals surrounding a star-shaped white center

Leaf: narrowly lance-shaped, grayish-green leaves, ½–1" (1–2.5 cm) long, with fuzzy short white hairs; thread-like sprawling stem

Bloom: Apr–Oct

Cycle/Origin: perennial; native

Zone/Habitat: desert scrub and grasslands at 2,200–5,000' (670–1,525 m); along washes, roadsides, slopes, flats

Range: scattered locations throughout Arizona, but mainly in a band from the northwestern to the south-eastern corners, covering two-thirds of the state

Notes: A stunningly beautiful, commonly seen wildflower of the deserts, the flowers and stems appear too delicate to grow in such a harsh environment. The slightest touch bruises the flower, yet the slim stem sprawls along the ground or climbs the nearest plant or rock for support, as if not bothered by the arid heat. Also called Arizona blue eyes for the flower's round shape and blue color of a human eye. Similar to the nonnative slender morning glory (*E. alsinoides*) (not shown), which also occurs in southern Arizona, it has compound leaves with round leaflets and smaller flowers.

FLOWER TYPE **Regular**   LEAF TYPE **Simple**   LEAF ATTACHMENT **Alternate**

Bird's Bill Dayflower

Commelina dianthifolia

Family: Spiderwort (Commelinaceae)

Height: 6–15" (15–38 cm)

Flower: intensely blue flowers, 1" (2.5 cm) wide, with 3 triangular petals and yellow-tipped flower parts; each bloom is held in a large, folded, boat-shaped green bract

Leaf: narrow grass-like blades, 2–6" (5–15 cm) long, alternating along and clasping the stem

Bloom: Jul–Sep

Cycle/Origin: perennial; native

Zone/Habitat: oak/pinyon pine/juniper woodlands, montane, subalpine at 4,000–9,500' (1,220–2,895 m); clearings among pines or other conifers, meadows

Range: eastern three-quarters of Arizona

Notes: Called "dayflower" for the flower's habit of opening early in the morning and wilting by noon, this showy wildflower is most commonly seen among ponderosa pines and is easily found in late summer blooming on Mount Lemmon in the Santa Catalina Mountains, just north of Tucson. Often cultivated for its unusual blue flowers, it can be grown from seed and blooms in the first year. It's a good plant for rock gardens, containers, and borders. It's hardy in temperatures down to 18°F (-8°C), but it needs extra water in arid areas in the West.

FLOWER TYPE
Regular

LEAF TYPE
Simple

LEAF ATTACHMENT
Alternate

LEAF ATTACHMENT
Clasping

27

Long-flowered Gilia
Ipomopsis longiflora

Family: Phlox (Polemoniaceae)

Height: 4–24" (10–61 cm)

Flower: star-shaped, tubular, whitish-blue flower, 1–2" (2.5–5 cm) long; petals are fused into a narrow, long reddish tube and spread into 5 pointed lobes veined with purple; flower has a white center

Leaf: thread-like stem leaves, ½–2½" (1–6 cm) long, are bright green; lower leaves are divided into lobes; basal leaves wither before the plant flowers

Fruit: oval green capsule, turning brown, ⅓" (0.8 cm) long

Bloom: May–Nov, after rainfall

Cycle/Origin: annual, biennial; native

Zone/Habitat: all life zones except riparian deciduous at 2,000–9,500' (610–2,745 m); canyons, limestone soils

Range: throughout, except the southwestern corner

Notes: One of 14 species of *Ipomopsis* in Arizona, long-flowered gilia is very common near Greer and Springerville in northeastern Arizona, occurring along roads in thick groups of 50–60 plants. It's also called blue gilia or blue starflower for the overall bluish appearance of the purple-veined petals. The light color of the slender flowers, the thin stems, and thread-like leaves make this plant hard to spot and make it appear too fragile for the harsh desert habitat, where it can also be found.

FLOWER TYPE
Tube

LEAF TYPE
Simple Lobed

LEAF ATTACHMENT
Alternate

LEAF ATTACHMENT
Basal

FRUIT
Pod

Prairie Spiderwort
Tradescantia occidentalis

Family: Spiderwort (Commelinaceae)

Height: 10–30" (25–76 cm)

Flower: cluster of up to 10 flowers, each 1–2" (2.5–5 cm) wide, with 3 violet-blue petals surrounding a golden-yellow center; flowers open only a few at a time and are sometimes pink to white

Leaf: grass-like, arching, bluish-green leaves, 6–15" (15–37.5 cm) long, clasp the stem at the base; each leaf has long parallel veining and is folded lengthwise, forming a V-groove

Bloom: Apr–Sep

Cycle/Origin: perennial; native

Zone/Habitat: grasslands, oak/pinyon pine/juniper woods, montane at 3,000–7,000' (915–2,135 m); along roads

Range: throughout, except the northwestern corner

Notes: This unusual-looking plant has exotic-looking flowers that open in the morning and often wilt by noon on hot days. "Spider" comes from several characteristics unique to the plant. One is the angular leaf attachment, suggestive of the legs of a sitting spider; another is the stringy, mucilaginous sap that strings out like a spider's web when the leaf is torn apart. "Wort" is derived from *wyrt*, an Old English word for "plant." Flowers change from blue to purple when exposed to air pollution, thus it has recently been used as a natural barometer for air quality.

FLOWER TYPE	LEAF TYPE	LEAF ATTACHMENT	LEAF ATTACHMENT
Regular	**Simple**	**Alternate**	**Clasping**

Western Blue Flax
Linum lewisii

Family: Flax (Linaceae)

Height: 12–36" (30–91 cm)

Flower: sky blue-to-lavender flowers, 1–2" (2.5–5 cm) wide, have 5 broad fan-shaped petals around a greenish center; blossoms last only 1 day

Leaf: narrowly lance-shaped or thread-like, bluish-green leaves, ½–1" (1–2.5 cm) long, with sharply pointed tips, mostly alternate, some opposite or whorled; stems densely leafy

Bloom: Apr–Nov, flowers profusely over 6 weeks

Cycle/Origin: perennial; native

Zone/Habitat: grasslands, oak/pinyon pine/juniper woodlands and montane at 3,200–9,000' (975–2,745 m); among ponderosa pines, disturbed rocky ground

Range: northern half of Arizona, scattered in the southern half of the state

Notes: *Linum* is from an old Greek name for "flax" and *lewisii* is for Meriwether Lewis of the Lewis and Clark Expedition, who explored the American West in the early 1800s, covering nearly 8,000 miles (12,880 km) by boat, horseback, and on foot. Although not a botanist, he and William Clark brought back this pretty blue wildflower and many other plant species. Widespread throughout the West and Midwest, it's sometimes called prairie flax; its flowers can also be white.

FLOWER TYPE
Regular

LEAF TYPE
Simple

LEAF ATTACHMENT
Alternate

LEAF ATTACHMENT
Opposite

LEAF ATTACHMENT
Whorl

Chia
Salvia columbariae

Family: Mint (Lamiaceae)

Height: 4–20" (10–50 cm)

Flower: round cluster, 1–2" (2.5–5 cm) wide, of tiny flowers of neon blue to pale blue with spine-tipped maroon bracts below; sometimes 1 cluster at top of stem, often 2–4 clusters surround the stem at intervals; flowers have a skunk-like odor

Leaf: oblong basal leaves, 1–4" (2.5–10 cm) long, are thick, wrinkled, sticky, with deep irregular rounded lobes, tiny grayish bristles above; few smaller stem leaves found only on lowest part of square stem

Bloom: Mar–May

Cycle/Origin: annual; native

Zone/Habitat: desert scrub, grasslands interior chaparral below 3,500' (1,065 m); slopes, dry disturbed soils

Range: two-thirds of Arizona, in a wide band from the northwestern to southeastern corners of the state

Notes: Native Americans have cultivated this plant along with corn; large plots of chia still flower where some ancient villages once stood. Indigenous Peoples have eaten the nutritious nut-flavored seeds and have made a minty beverage of ground seeds mixed with water. The tiny nutlets were soaked in water to make a sticky poultice used to treat fevers and wounds. Chia is a traditional food useful in treating diabetes.

CLUSTER TYPE
Round

FLOWER TYPE
Irregular

LEAF TYPE
Simple Lobed

LEAF ATTACHMENT
Opposite

LEAF ATTACHMENT
Basal

Blue Bonnet Lupine
Lupinus palmeri

Family: Pea or Bean (Fabaceae)

Height: 13–16" (33–40 cm)

Flower: cylindrical dense spike, 3–4½" (7.5–11 cm) long, of many pea-like, blue-to-purple flowers; each flower, ⅓" (.8 cm) long, appears to have 3 petals but actually has 5 petals fused together

Leaf: each hand-shaped leaf, 2½" (6 cm) wide, has 5–8 slender, pointed oval leaflets; leaves on long, velvety, grayish-green stems rising mostly from the base

Fruit: pea-like green pod, turning tan, ¾" (2 cm) long, is oval and flat, covered with short fuzzy hairs

Bloom: Apr–Oct

Cycle/Origin: perennial; native

Zone/Habitat: montane at 6,000–8,000' (1,830–2,440 m); under ponderosa pines

Range: throughout, except the southwestern corner

Notes: This tall, showy species is the most common lupine in the ponderosa pine forests of the montane life zone. The spike cluster blooms from the bottom up, with the newer flowers a light blue and older flowers turning a deep blue. The leaflets are grayish green and outlined with a smooth gray margin. Lupines are able to grow in poor or disturbed soils since they have the ability to fix nitrogen from the air, which adds to the fertility of the soil.

CLUSTER TYPE
Spike

FLOWER TYPE
Irregular

LEAF TYPE
Palmate

LEAF ATTACHMENT
Alternate

LEAF ATTACHMENT
Basal

FRUIT
Pod

Barestem Larkspur

Delphinium scaposum

Family: Buttercup (Ranunculaceae)

Height: 10–24" (25–61 cm)

Flower: open loose spike, 5–12" (13–30 cm) long, flowers of sky blue to royal blue, 1" (2.5 cm) wide; each bloom has 5 blue sepals (upper sepal with long backward-curving purple spur) and 3 smaller blue petals (erect fourth petal is white)

Leaf: mostly basal, long-stalked leaves, shaped like a half circle, ½–2½" (1–6 cm) wide, with flat bases and deeply divided into 5 irregular-toothed lobes

Fruit: narrow brown seedpod, ½" (1 cm) long, 3-parted

Bloom: Feb–May

Cycle/Origin: perennial; native

Zone/Habitat: desert scrub, grasslands, oak/pinyon pine/juniper woodlands below 5,000' (1,525 m); mesas, hills

Range: throughout Arizona, except the southwestern and southeastern corners

Notes: *Scaposum*, Latin for "stem" or "scape" in the name is for the nearly leafless flower stalk. Flowers at the bottom of the spike open first. In spring, hike King's Canyon Trail in the Tucson Mountains, north of the famous Arizona-Sonoran Desert Museum, to see this spectacular wildflower. Parts of the plant have been made into a wash that has been used by Navajo or Hopi mothers following childbirth.

CLUSTER TYPE
Spike

FLOWER TYPE
Irregular

LEAF TYPE
Simple Lobed

LEAF ATTACHMENT
Basal

FRUIT
Pod

Desert Larkspur
Delphinium parishii

Family: Buttercup (Ranunculaceae)

Height: 7–24" (18–61 cm)

Flower: open loose spike, 5–16" (13–40 cm) long, with scattered flowers of sky blue to dark lavender, 1" (2.5 cm) wide; blooms have 5 petal-like pointed sepals (upper sepal with a long backward-curving purple spur) and 4 smaller hairy petals

Leaf: grayish-green leaves, ½–3" (1–7.5 cm) wide, deeply divided into irregular narrow pointed lobes and growing on long stalks from lower third or base of stem; most leaves wither by the time plant blooms

Fruit: narrow long brown seedpod, ¾" (2 cm) long

Bloom: Feb–Jun

Cycle/Origin: perennial; native

Zone/Habitat: desert scrub below 5,000' (1,525 m); arroyos

Range: south-central and northwestern Arizona, combined to include about half of the state

Notes: The most drought-tolerant larkspur in the United States, the size and number of leaves vary according to climate. It can be found along washes in the Silverbell Mountains in Ironwood Forest National Monument, west of Tucson. All the plant parts contain poisonous alkaloids and should never be eaten or even handled by people. It's fatal to livestock if consumed in large amounts.

CLUSTER TYPE | FLOWER TYPE | LEAF TYPE | LEAF ATTACHMENT | LEAF ATTACHMENT | FRUIT
Spike | **Irregular** | **Simple Lobed** | **Alternate** | **Basal** | **Pod**

hairy petals

Arroyo Lupine
Lupinus sparsiflorus

Family: Pea or Bean (Fabaceae)

Height: 8–16" (20–40 cm)

Flower: sparse spike cluster, 6–8" (15–20 cm) long, of pea-like blue flowers, each ½" (1 cm) long; upper petal (standard) has a yellow spot, lower petals (keel) have darker blue streaks and are slightly hairy below

Leaf: each leaf has 5–11 narrow, pointed, fuzzy leaflets arranged in a finger-like spread; leaves are 1–1½" (2.5–4 cm) wide, on stems rising mostly from the base

Fruit: green seedpod, turning beige, 1½" (4 cm) long, grows horizontally from the spike

Bloom: Jan–May

Cycle/Origin: annual; native

Zone/Habitat: desert scrub, grasslands at 100–3,000' (30–915 m); flats, lower mountain slopes (bajadas), mesas

Range: two-thirds of Arizona, in a wide band from the northwestern to southeastern parts of the state

Notes: "Arroyo" is Spanish for "creek," referring to a dry streambed (wash) through which water flows intermittently, along which this plant is often found. In years with good winter rains, arroyo lupine has some of the desert's most conspicuous blooms. Like all lupines, the leaflets turn to face the sun throughout the day, maximizing the amount of sunlight the plant absorbs.

CLUSTER TYPE
Spike

FLOWER TYPE
Irregular

LEAF TYPE
Palmate

LEAF ATTACHMENT
Alternate

LEAF ATTACHMENT
Basal

FRUIT
Pod

43

Columbian Monkshood
Aconitum columbianum

Family: Buttercup (Ranunculaceae)

Height: 1–7' (0.3–21 m)

Flower: very open spike clusters, 6–22" (15–56 cm) long, flowers of dark blue to velvet purple, 1" (2.5 cm) long; blooms have 5 petal-like sepals with the uppermost forming a high arching "hood," 2 backward-curving side "wings," and 2 forming the split bottom lip; center of green flower parts

Leaf: wide, hand-shaped, dark-green leaves, 1–7" (2.5–18 cm) wide, have 3–5 deep, wedge-shaped lobes with toothed or jaggedly lobed edges; hollow stem

Fruit: vase-shaped pods, ½" (1 cm) long, have black seeds

Bloom: Jun–Sep

Cycle/Origin: perennial; native

Zone/Habitat: riparian deciduous, montane, subalpine at 5,000–10,000' (1,525–3,050 m); along mountain streams

Range: northern half and southeastern corner of Arizona

Notes: The foliage is frequently hidden, with only the spike of blue flowers rising above other vegetation. Usually grows as tall as 3 feet (.9 m), but can grow taller. Found throughout the West and as far north as Alaska; in Arizona, it is limited to the cooler mountains, wherever moist soils are present. *Aconitum* means "unconquerable poison." Most species in the genus are, in fact, extremely poisonous.

CLUSTER TYPE
Spike

FLOWER TYPE
Irregular

LEAF TYPE
Simple Lobed

LEAF ATTACHMENT
Alternate

FRUIT
Pod

Canaigre Dock
Rumex hymenosepalus

Family: Buckwheat (Polygonaceae)

Height: 2–4' (61–122 cm)

Flower: dense spike cluster, 12" (30 cm) long, is pointed at the tip and widest in the middle; cluster made up of many tiny, pinkish-green flowers; each flower has heart-shaped sepals and petals

Leaf: basal leaves, 3–12" (7.5–30 cm) long, are arching, tongue-shaped, and have long, stout, and succulent stalks

Fruit: 3-sided, heart-shaped winged capsule, ⅓" (0.8 cm) long, is green, turning red at maturity

Bloom: middle Feb–Apr at lower elevations, until June at medium elevations

Cycle/Origin: perennial; native

Zone/Habitat: desert scrub, grasslands, riparian deciduous, 1,000–6,000' (305–1,830 m); fallow fields, alkaline soils

Range: throughout Arizona, except the southwestern and southeastern corners of the state

Notes: The very large basal leaves produced in the spring were historically cooked as greens, thus its other common name, wild rhubarb. It sends up a stout, conspicuous flower stalk covered with tiny pinkish-green flowers, which are followed by showy, heart-shaped seed capsules that turn pink or red when mature. canaigre dock contains large amounts of tannin, which is useful in making leather products. Also called tanner's dock.

CLUSTER TYPE	FLOWER TYPE	LEAF TYPE	LEAF ATTACHMENT	FRUIT
Spike	**Irregular**	**Simple**	**Basal**	**Pod**

Elkweed
Frasera speciosa

Family: Gentian (Gentianaceae)

Height: 2–6' (0.6–1.8 m)

Flower: tall, cylindrical, whitish-green spikes, 2–6' (.6–1.8 m) long, made up of densely packed, star-shaped flowers; each bloom, 1½" (4 cm) wide, has 4 greenish (flecked with purple) petals with fringed glands

Leaf: long oval basal leaves, 6–12" (15–30 cm) long, fuzzy below, thick with smooth edges; stalk has many leaves in whorls of 4–6, upper leaves smaller

Bloom: May–Aug

Cycle/Origin: perennial; native

Zone/Habitat: all life zones except desert scrub at 5,000–10,000' (1,525–3,050 m); among conifers or aspens, along roads, sunny grassy hillsides, rocky slopes, rich soils

Range: northern half and southeastern corner of Arizona

Notes: Sometimes called deer ears for the long oval leaves, this is one of the most conspicuous and common mountain plants. The species name *speciosa* means "showy" and refers to its tall, stout flower spikes, thus another name, monument plant. Colonies of these plants flower all at the same time, but only every few years. Each elkweed has a very large basal rosette of leaves for most of its lifetime of 20–80 years and sends up the large flowering spike only once, then dies. The decaying, fallen flowering stalk then provides shelter and nutrition for its own seedlings, enabling them to survive.

CLUSTER TYPE
Spike

FLOWER TYPE
Regular

LEAF TYPE
Simple

LEAF ATTACHMENT
Whorl

LEAF ATTACHMENT
Basal

maroon
anthers

Caliche Globe Mallow
Sphaeralcea laxa

Family: Mallow (Malvaceae)

Height: 12–36" (30–91 cm)

Flower: loose spike cluster, 6–12" (15–30 cm) long, of slightly cupped, bright reddish-orange flowers, 1–1½" (2.5–4 cm) wide; 5 slightly wrinkled, fan-shaped petals surround a star-shaped green center with dark maroon male flower parts (anthers)

Leaf: 3-lobed, triangular or heart-shaped, grayish-green leaves, ½–2" (1–5 cm) long, have scalloped edges; tiny star-shaped white hairs on leaves and stems

Fruit: pod-like tan container, ¼" (.6 cm) wide, shaped like half an orange, has 12–14 pie-shaped segments

Bloom: Mar–Nov, mostly in spring, but also after heavy rain

Cycle/Origin: perennial; native

Zone/Habitat: desert scrub and grasslands at 2,000–6,000' (610–1,830 m); flats, mesas

Range: eastern two-thirds of Arizona

Notes: It's the most common globe mallow found in the deserts near Tucson, but desert globe mallow (pg. 67) is most often cultivated in highway medians and landscaping in that area. Unlike desert globe mallow's orange anthers, caliche globe mallow anthers are always maroon or pink, while petal color varies from orange to pink, lavender, or white in both species (see inset). Grows in alkaline soils containing a hard layer of calcium carbonate (caliche) beneath the surface.

CLUSTER TYPE
Spike

FLOWER TYPE
Regular

LEAF TYPE
Simple Lobed

LEAF ATTACHMENT
Alternate

FRUIT
Pod

Southwestern Indian Paintbrush
Castilleja integra

Family: Broomrape (Orobanchaceae)

Height: 4–20" (10–51 cm)

Flower: spike cluster, 2–6" (2–12 cm) long, of tubular deep-green flowers, 1–1¾" (2.5–4.5 cm) long, protruding from fuzzy leafy bracts with 0–3 lobes; bracts are usually reddish orange, sometimes scarlet, salmon, or pale yellow; often mistaken for flower petals

Leaf: clasping, grayish-green-to-purplish leaves, ¾–2¾" (2–7 cm) long, hairy, narrow and pointed, undivided, usually not lobed, edges roll inward toward the center of the leaf

Fruit: small pod-like green container, ½" (1 cm) long

Bloom: Mar–Sep

Cycle/Origin: perennial; native

Zone/Habitat: dry rocky slopes, in grasslands and open forests, on ledges and road banks, valleys to subalpine at 3,280–10,827' (1,000–3,300 m); among pines or oaks

Range: most of Arizona, except southwestern corner

Notes: This short, shrubby, semiparasitic plant has erect stems densely covered in matted woolly hairs. The actual green flowers are tubular and protrude more conspicuously from the colored bracts than in other Indian paintbrushes. Unlike desert Indian paintbrush (pg. 205), the leaves are undivided, not lobed, thus another common name, wholeleaf Indian paintbrush. It's a host for the larvae of the Fulvia checkerspot butterfly, *Chlosyne fulvia*.

CLUSTER TYPE	FLOWER TYPE	LEAF TYPE	LEAF ATTACHMENT	FRUIT
Spike	**Tube**	**Simple**	**Alternate**	**Pod**

Thurber Desert-honeysuckle
Anisacanthus thurberi

Family: Acanthus (Acanthaceae)

Height: 3–6' (0.9–1.8 m); shrub

Flower: slim, tubular reddish-orange or orange flowers, 1–2" (2.5–5 cm) long, have fused petals flaring into 4 long pointed lobes that curl backward, protruding orange-and-white flower parts, and green sepals

Leaf: stalkless elliptical leaves, 1–2½" (2.5–6 cm) long, with smooth edges and pointed tips; usually in dense clusters

Bloom: Mar–Jun and Oct–Dec

Cycle/Origin: perennial; native

Zone/Habitat: desert scrub, interior chaparral, oak/pinyon pine/juniper woods, riparian deciduous at 1,500–5,500' (460–1,675 m); canyons, along washes

Range: throughout Arizona, except the north-central part of the state

Notes: This common flowering shrub is found only in Arizona and New Mexico in the United States, but it ranges south into northern Mexico. Also called chuparosa, meaning "hummingbird" in Spanish, the name is commonly used for all plants that attract hummingbirds. There are more species of hummingbirds found in Arizona than in any other state, making planting flowers for these tiny "jewels" popular. A good choice for wildlife gardens, it requires well-drained soil, a little water, and full sun; it's hardy to 15°F (-9°C).

FLOWER TYPE	LEAF TYPE	LEAF ATTACHMENT	LEAF ATTACHMENT
Tube	**Simple**	**Opposite**	**Whorl**

Orange Sneezeweed

Hymenoxys hoopesii

Family: Aster (Asteraceae)

Height: 1–3' (30–91 cm); shrub

Flower: clusters of 1–12 yellow-to-orange flower heads, each large, showy bloom, 1–3" (2.5–7.6 cm) wide, made of 14–26 long, drooping petals (ray flowers) circling a mounded yellow center (disk flowers); petal tips often 3-lobed

Leaf: upright, lance-shaped, gland-dotted leaves, 1–6" (2.5–15 cm) long, larger at base of plant, becoming smaller upward on 1–4 woolly green or greenish-purple stems that branch toward top of plant

Bloom: Jun–Sep

Cycle/Origin: perennial, native

Zone/Habitat: rich moist soils in mountain meadows; pine, spruce, aspen, and fir forests, and along streams at 7,000–1,100' (2,134–3,353 m)

Range: the mountains of southern, eastern, and northern Arizona

Notes: Sometimes called owl-claws, this robust plant has long-blooming flowers that attract bees, butterflies, and moths. Avoided by rabbits, the leaves contain toxins that make them also unpalatable to cows and sheep. Historically, the crushed flowers were used to make a yellow dye. With similar-looking flowers, cut-leaf coneflower, (pg. 331), is found in the same range and habitat, but cutleaf leaves have deeply cut, pointed lobes, and the center of the bloom protrudes in a column above the petals.

FLOWER TYPE   LEAF TYPE   LEAF ATTACHMENT
Composite   **Simple**   **Alternate**

Hummingbird's Trumpet
Epilobium canum

Family: Evening-primrose (Onagraceae)

Height: 12–24" (30–61 cm); shrub

Flower: bright-orange tubular flowers, 1½" (4 cm) long, flaring at mouth into 4 wrinkled petals and protruding reddish-orange flower parts; each petal is notched in the center; flowers grouped toward top of stems

Leaf: elliptical, dark-green leaves, ½–2" (1–5 cm) long, are hairy, sticky, with edges finely toothed; lower leaves opposite, upper leaves alternate and much smaller

Fruit: cylindrical beaked hairy capsule, 1" (2.5 cm) long

Bloom: Jun–Dec

Cycle/Origin: perennial; native

Zone/Habitat: interior chaparral, oak/pinyon pine/juniper woods, riparian deciduous at 2,500–7,000' (760–2,135 m); moist seeps, rocky slopes, canyons, arroyos

Range: throughout Arizona, except the northeastern and southwestern corners of the state

Notes: A hummingbird magnet, this flower is often grown in desert wildlife gardens in moist soil near birdbaths or along a water feature. Can tolerate drier conditions in cooler climates. In the wild, it is easily found in the fall along washes in Molino Basin and Bear Canyon in the Santa Catalina Mountains, north of Tucson. Hummingbirds defend these rich nectar sources from each other, competing for territories with the most blooms.

FLOWER TYPE
Tube

LEAF TYPE
Simple

LEAF ATTACHMENT
Alternate

LEAF ATTACHMENT
Opposite

FRUIT
Pod

Firewheel

Gaillardia pulchella

Family: Aster (Asteraceae)

Height: 2–24" (5–61 cm)

Flower: daisy-like, tricolored flower head, 2–3" (5–7.5 cm) wide, made up of 8–14 triangular (orange, red, or purple) petals with 3-lobed (usually yellow or orange) tips surrounding a domed maroon center

Leaf: narrowly oblong or spoon-shaped leaves, ½–3½" (1–9 cm) long, are fuzzy above with usually smooth edges; upper leaves smaller and clasping; alternately attached to multibranched, sticky-haired stem

Bloom: Apr–Sep

Cycle/Origin: usually annual, sometimes perennial or biennial; native

Zone/Habitat: grasslands, pinyon pine/juniper woodlands, montane at 3,500–6,000' (1,065–1,830 m); disturbed ground, along roads and railroads, forest clearings

Range: eastern half of Arizona

Notes: Called firewheel because the flower resembles a child's pinwheel, its maroon center is surrounded by an orange or red ring that, in turn, is encircled by a ring of yellow. It readily self-seeds and forms large colorful masses of flowers that blanket the ground. Many state highway departments plant this eye-catching flower along roads. It's often grown in wildflower gardens since it needs little care and the flowers last a long time.

FLOWER TYPE   LEAF TYPE   LEAF ATTACHMENT
Composite   **Simple**   **Alternate**

fruit

Butterflyweed
Asclepias tuberosa

Family: Dogbane (Apocynaceae)

Height: 12–24" (30–61 cm)

Flower: large flat cluster, 2–3" (5–7.5 cm) wide, of small, deep-orange flowers; each ⅜" (0.9 cm) wide, with downward-curving petals; flower color varies from all yellow to red

Leaf: hairy lance-shaped leaves, 2–6" (5–15 cm) long, widen near tips and are toothless; hairy stem

Fruit: erect narrow green pod, turning brown, 6" (15 cm) long, is covered with fine hairs; pods are in small clusters and have large brown seeds with silken "parachutes" to carry away each seed

Bloom: May–Sep

Cycle/Origin: perennial; native

Zone/Habitat: grasslands and montane at 4,000–8,000' (1,220–1,830 m); clearings in pine forests

Range: northern half and southeastern part of Arizona

Notes: Also called butterfly milkweed, although it lacks milky sap. Found in clumps, the species name *tuberosa* refers to its large taproot, which makes it nearly impossible to transplant. Can be grown from seed. Single stems branch only near the top, and flower clusters harbor up to 25 flowers. Roots and stems have been used in folk medicine. A host plant for gray hairstreak and monarch butterfly caterpillars.

CLUSTER TYPE	FLOWER TYPE	LEAF TYPE	LEAF ATTACHMENT	FRUIT
Flat	**Irregular**	**Simple**	**Alternate**	**Pod**

yellow form

Desert Mariposa Lily
Calochortus kennedyi

Family: Lily (Liliaceae)

Height: 4–16" (10–40 cm)

Flower: bright-orange flower, 3" (7.5 cm) wide; 3 broad petals, each with fringed blotch at base; 3 narrow sepals; purple-and-orange hairy center

Leaf: basal leaves, 4–8" (10–20 cm) long, are grass-like, folded lengthwise and wither before the plant blooms; few stem leaves

Fruit: lance-shaped capsule, 1½–2½" (4–6 cm) long, is purplish green with white stripes and turns brown

Bloom: Mar–May, after good winter rains

Cycle/Origin: perennial; native

Zone/Habitat: desert scrub and grasslands at 2,000–5,000' (610–1,525 m); open or brushy areas, hillsides, flats

Range: western third and southernmost quarter of Arizona

Notes: "Mariposa" means "butterfly" in Spanish and refers to the wing-like movement of the colorful petals in a breeze. It grows on dry rocky hillsides. It's often mistaken by springtime hikers for the four-petaled California poppy (pg. 363) from a distance, but the flowers of desert mariposa lily are larger and have three petals. The less common, yellow-flowered variation of desert mariposa lily may be mistaken for golden mariposa lily (*C. aureus*) (not shown), which has a thin dark crescent on the petal bases and is less hairy in the flower center.

FLOWER TYPE
Regular

LEAF TYPE
Simple

LEAF ATTACHMENT
Alternate

LEAF ATTACHMENT
Basal

FRUIT
Pod

orange anthers

Desert Globe Mallow

Sphaeralcea ambigua

Family: Mallow (Malvaceae)

Height: 20–36" (50–91 cm)

Flower: wand-like spike cluster, 6–12" (15–30 cm) long, of many bowl-shaped, light-orange flowers, ⅝–2" (1.5–5 cm) wide; 5 triangular orange petals with pale-yellow bases and wavy outer edges surround a green center with yellow male flower parts (anthers)

Leaf: triangular, grayish-green leaves, ⅝–2" (1.5–5 cm) long, are deeply veined, 3-lobed, and have scalloped margins; upper leaves much smaller; star-shaped white hairs cover leaves and stems

Fruit: pod-like tan container, ¼" (0.6 cm) wide, shaped like half an orange, is segmented and has tiny seeds

Bloom: mostly Mar–Apr, any time of year after heavy rain

Cycle/Origin: perennial; native

Zone/Habitat: desert scrub below 3,500' (1,065 m); sandy washes

Range: western two-thirds of Arizona

Notes: It's the most common globe mallow found east of Phoenix and along the Pinal Pioneer Parkway (Highway 79) from Tucson to Florence, Arizona. Flowers can be white, pale pink, lavender, or red; the male flower parts (anthers) are always yellow. It grows in many-stemmed clumps with showy flower stalks above the mound of foliage. Bighorn sheep and domestic sheep and goats eat the leaves.

CLUSTER TYPE
Spike

FLOWER TYPE
Regular

LEAF TYPE
Simple Lobed

LEAF ATTACHMENT
Alternate

FRUIT
Pod

Small-flowered Globe Mallow
Sphaeralcea parvifolia

Family: Mallow (Malvaceae)

Height: 24–36" (61–91 cm)

Flower: straight spike cluster, 12–18" (30–45 cm) long, of whorls of many cup-shaped, bright-orange flowers, 1" (2.5 cm) wide; 5 heart-shaped orange petals with pale-yellow bases surround a green center with yellow male flower parts (anthers)

Leaf: small, broadly triangular, grayish-green leaves, ½–1½" (1–4 cm) long, have extremely wavy margins; upper surfaces have white glands and deep veins

Fruit: flattened, disk-shaped pod is green, turning tan, ¼" (0.6 cm) wide, and is segmented

Bloom: May–Sep

Cycle/Origin: perennial; native

Zone/Habitat: desert scrub, oak/pinyon pine/juniper woodlands, 3,500–7,000' (1,065–2,135 m); low canyons

Range: northern half of Arizona

Notes: Especially common in canyon country such as the Four Corners area of northeastern Arizona, it often forms dense colonies. Although heat and drought tolerant, in years following heavy winter rains it blooms for weeks, carpeting large areas along roads with orange. The Latin *parvifolia* means "little leaf" and fits this plant to a T, as the curly leaves are the smallest among globe mallows in the state.

CLUSTER TYPE
Spike

FLOWER TYPE
Regular

LEAF TYPE
Simple Lobed

LEAF ATTACHMENT
Alternate

FRUIT
Pod

Bajada Lupine
Lupinus concinnus

Family: Pea or Bean (Fabaceae)

Height: 4–12" (10–30 cm)

Flower: dense pinkish-purple spike, 1–3½" (2.5–9 cm) long, has pea-like flowers, ¼–½" (0.6–1 cm) long, in a spiral; bloom has an upper petal (banner) spotted with yellowish white; lower petal (keel) is faintly streaked darker blue; several spikes per plant

Leaf: round, densely hairy, grayish-green basal leaves, 1–1½" (2.5–4 cm) wide, divided into 5–9 narrow oval leaflets; leaves on hairy stems, sprawling or erect

Fruit: hairy tan seedpod, ⅝" (1.5 cm) long, has 3–5 seeds

Bloom: Mar–May

Cycle/Origin: annual; native

Zone/Habitat: desert scrub below 5,000' (1,525 m); lower mountain slopes (bajadas), burned areas, sandy soils

Range: throughout, except the southwestern corner

Notes: "Bajada" is Spanish for "slope," where these low-growing hairy plants are often found, and refers to fan-shaped debris deposited by floodwaters rushing out of a mountain canyon. The plant is common in sandy soils throughout the Southwest, from southern California to western Texas and south into Mexico. In springtime following heavy winter rains, it lines the roadsides of the Pinal Pioneer Parkway from Tucson to Florence, Arizona. *Concinnus* means elegant; also called elegant lupine.

CLUSTER TYPE	FLOWER TYPE	LEAF TYPE	LEAF ATTACHMENT	FRUIT
Spike	**Irregular**	**Palmate**	**Basal**	**Pod**

Spreading Dogbane
Apocynum androsaemifolium

Family: Dogbane (Apocynaceae)

Height: 12–20" (30–50 cm)

Flower: groups of 2–10 pink-to-white flowers on stalks above leaves; each bell-shaped flower, ⅓" (.8 cm) long, can be white with pink stripes within the bell

Leaf: oval leaves, 2–4" (5–10 cm) long, pale whitish green and slightly hairy below, toothless wavy margins

Fruit: thin pod, 3–8" (7.5–20 cm) long, opens along 1 side, revealing seeds attached to long tufts of white fuzz

Bloom: Jun–Aug

Cycle/Origin: perennial; native

Zone/Habitat: interior chaparral, riparian deciduous, montane at 7,000–9,000' (2,135–2,745 m); clearings, slopes

Range: northern half and southeastern part of Arizona

Notes: This perennial has a single main stem branching into many "spreading" stems. A close relative of the milkweed, it produces a thick white milky juice in its stems and leaves. This juice contains cardiac glycosides, which cause hot flashes, rapid heartbeat, and fatigue. Five thin sensitive scales in the flower's throat ooze sweet nectar, which attracts flies. The scale will turn inward when a fly brushes against it, trapping the insect. When dried and peeled, the fibrous bark makes a strong cord, which was once used by Native Americans for fishing and trapping. The same fibers are selectively used by orioles as nest-building material.

FLOWER TYPE **Bell**   LEAF TYPE **Simple**   LEAF ATTACHMENT **Opposite**   FRUIT **Pod**

73

Tenleaf Wood Sorrel
Oxalis decaphylla

Family: Wood Sorrel (Oxalidaceae)

Height: 3–5" (7.5–13 cm)

Flower: pink flowers, ½" (1 cm) wide, with yellow throats; each bloom has 5 broad, streaked petals that are pink on outer half and fused at the white base, curving out around a white-and-yellow center

Leaf: basal leaves, 2" (5 cm) wide, appearing like a closed umbrella, are divided into 4–10 folded heart-shaped leaflets hung upside down by tips from a central point on a long stalk; leaflets are green and edged with maroon above, and are maroon below

Bloom: Jun–Aug

Cycle/Origin: perennial; native

Zone/Habitat: oak/pinyon pine/juniper woodlands, montane and subalpine at 5,000–9,500' (1,525–2,895 m); among grasses in moist, deep loamy soils

Range: southeastern quarter of Arizona, and the northern half of the state, except the northwestern corner

Notes: The bulbs of this plant make up a large portion of the diet of the Montezuma quail, which is dependent upon tenleaf wood sorrel being plentiful in its habitat. This colorful quail is found in Arizona and New Mexico, the only two states in the US where this plant is known to occur. Foliage of plants in the genus *Oxalis* contains oxalic acid, which is secreted as sharp calcium oxalate crystals.

FLOWER TYPE
Regular

LEAF TYPE
Compound

LEAF ATTACHMENT
Basal

Pineywoods Geranium
Geranium caespitosum

Family: Geranium (Geraniaceae)

Height: 4–36" (10–91 cm)

Flower: pink-to-lilac flower, ½" (1 cm) wide, has 5 drooping petals with dark-pink veins, 5 sepals with thread-like tips, greenish flower parts

Leaf: hand-shaped hairy basal leaves, 1½" (4 cm) wide, pinkish edges, 5 toothed lobes; red stems

Fruit: stiff green container, ½" (1 cm) long, shaped like a crane's bill, contains 1 seed tipped with an elongated tail that coils at maturity

Bloom: May–Oct

Cycle/Origin: perennial; native

Zone/Habitat: montane at 6,000–9,000' (1,830–2,745 m); among ponderosa pines, meadows, along trails, dry soils

Range: northern half and southeastern corner of Arizona

Notes: Species name *caespitosum* is Latin for "growing in clumps" and describes how this small plant is found. Genus name *Geranium* is from the Greek *geranos*, meaning "crane," and refers to the shape of the fruit, which resembles a crane's bill. The seed has a tail that coils at maturity and straightens out with rainfall, which forces the pointed seed into the soil. The leaves are fragrant when crushed. Indigenous Peoples have made a concoction from the root to treat diarrhea. It's different from Richardson geranium (pg. 235), which prefers moist soils, has white petals, and is purple veined.

FLOWER TYPE
Regular

LEAF TYPE
Simple Lobed

LEAF ATTACHMENT
Opposite

LEAF ATTACHMENT
Basal

FRUIT
Pod

77

Eastern Mojave Buckwheat
Eriogonum fasciculatum

Family: Buckwheat (Polygonaceae)

Height: 1–5' (30–152 cm); shrub

Flower: numerous fuzzy pink-to-white flowers in a densely packed flat cluster, ½–8" (1–20 cm) wide; each tiny flower is only ⅛" (0.3 cm) wide

Leaf: leathery narrow oblong leaves, ¼–½" (0.6–1 cm) long, with margins rolled inward; 1 to many leaves at each node of stem; reddish-brown stems erect or sprawling, turning grayish and woody with age

Bloom: Feb–Jun

Cycle/Origin: perennial; native

Zone/Habitat: desert scrub and grasslands at 1,000–4,500' (305–1,370 m); along roads and washes, slopes

Range: western two-thirds of Arizona

Notes: Many butterflies feed on the nectar of eastern Mojave buckwheat, and several species of butterfly caterpillars are dependent upon the foliage. Wild bees and honeybees also visit the flower, and it is an important wild nectar source used for honey production. Often cultivated in rock or butterfly gardens, this small, open, multistemmed shrub is easily grown from seed. Native Americans have used the plant medicinally to treat a variety of illnesses, including heart problems. Scientific studies have proven other species in the *Eriogonum* genus contain compounds that are beneficial to the heart. It's also known as California buckwheat.

CLUSTER TYPE | FLOWER TYPE | LEAF TYPE | LEAF ATTACHMENT
Flat | **Regular** | **Simple** | **Alternate**

Prairie Smoke
Geum triflorum

Family: Rose (Rosaceae)

Height: 6–20" (15–51 cm)

Flower: dark-pink, bell-shaped flowers, ½–¾" (1.3–2 cm) long, nodding in clusters of usually 3 (to as many as 9) blooms atop long stalks. Each flower made up of pale-yellow petals obscured and contained by rosy-pink sepals that are fused around the flower. Fuzzy stems have pairs of red leafy bracts that are deeply cleft below the flowers.

Leaf: dark-green, fern-like leaves, 3–7" (8–18 cm) long, covered in downy hairs and divided into 9–19 toothed leaflets

Bloom: May–Aug

Cycle/Origin: perennial; native

Zone/Habitat: among ponderosa pines and mixed conifers, in meadows, and along stream banks, upland prairie, 6,000–9,500' (1,830–2,900 m)

Range: northeastern third of Arizona

Notes: It's called prairie smoke for its eye-catching feathery-pink seedheads that appear to float above the forest floor. Flowers are nodding when blooming, but they become upright when fertilized and the ripe center bursts into silvery-pink, fuzzy plumes. Seedheads consist of long red threads with tiny seeds that disperse with the wind. It tolerates moderate shade and even fire and can be propagated via seed. The root tastes like sassafras and has been boiled into a tea by Native Americans to treat pain.

FLOWER TYPE
Bell

LEAF TYPE
Twice Compound

LEAF ATTACHMENT
Opposite

LEAF ATTACHMENT
Basal

Littleleaf Ratany
Krameria erecta

Family: Ratany (Krameriaceae)

Height: 12–36" (30–91 cm); shrub

Flower: dark-pink or purple flowers, ¾" (2 cm) wide, have 5 lance-shaped, fuzzy, pink petal-like sepals bent downward (lower sepal is cupped forward) around the tiny erect magenta petals with yellowish-green bases and protruding magenta or green flower parts

Leaf: fuzzy, whitish-green leaves, ⅛–½" (0.3–1 cm) long, are short and narrow with pointed tips and reddish prickles; oppositely attached along woody stems

Fruit: fuzzy, egg-shaped, greenish-cream pod, ½" (1 cm) long, has bright-red spines with minute barbs

Bloom: Apr–Nov

Cycle/Origin: perennial; native

Zone/Habitat: desert scrub, grasslands below 5,000' (1,525 m); rocky slopes and ridges, among grasses

Range: throughout Arizona, except the northeastern corner

Notes: This small, multibranched, sprawling gray shrub has inconspicuous leaves and oddly shaped flowers. All species in *Krameria* are semiparasitic, obtaining part of their nutrients through the roots of nearby plants. Instead of producing nectar, it attracts insect pollinators by making oil, which is collected by bees and mixed with pollen to make food for their larvae. The Tohono O'odham have extracted a red juice from the roots to make a dye.

FLOWER TYPE	LEAF TYPE	LEAF ATTACHMENT	FRUIT
Irregular	**Simple**	**Opposite**	**Pod**

83

Yellow-spine Thistle
Cirsium ochrocentrum

Family: Aster (Asteraceae)

Height: 12–36" (30–91 cm)

Flower: broad and rayless flower head, ¾–3" (2–7.5 cm) wide, is pink or red; bloom made of thin tubular disk flowers sitting on a spherical green base of very spiny bracts; spines point upward

Leaf: grayish-green basal leaves, 4–12" (10–30 cm) long, narrowly elliptical, covered with matted white hairs; each lobe or tooth ends in a long yellow spine; the bases of stem leaves form wings

Bloom: May–Oct

Cycle/Origin: perennial, biennial; native

Zone/Habitat: pinyon pine/juniper woods at 4,500–8,000' (1,370–2,440 m); roadsides, rangelands, disturbed areas, woodland clearings

Range: northern half and southern edge of Arizona

Notes: The long erect leaves grow close to the stem, allowing the densely hairy white undersides to be seen and making yellow-spine thistle easy to identify from a distance. One of the longest-spined thistles in Arizona, it also has the most spines. The flowers attract many types of insects. Traditionally, the peeled stems and the young leaves have been cooked and a tea was made by steeping the older leaves, and the roots were eaten raw or cooked. It spreads rapidly by its deep creeping roots and is considered a noxious weed in California.

FLOWER TYPE
Composite

LEAF TYPE
Simple Lobed

LEAF ATTACHMENT
Alternate

LEAF ATTACHMENT
Basal

Desert Five Spot
Eremalche rotundifolia

Family: Mallow (Malvaceae)

Height: 3–24" (7.5–61 cm)

Flower: spherical pink-to-purple flowers, 1" (2.5 cm) wide, of 5 round petals surrounding many yellow male flower parts (stamens); each petal is cream inside with a reddish blotch at the base

Leaf: round to heart-shaped, green or red leaves, ½–2½" (1–6 cm) wide, have short bristly hairs and irregularly scalloped edges, on long reddish leafstalks

Fruit: round disk-shaped tan pods, 1" (2.5 cm) wide, with 25–35 pie-shaped sections

Bloom: Mar–May

Cycle/Origin: annual; native

Zone/Habitat: desert scrub below 4,000' (1,220 m); flats, lower mountain slopes (bajadas), mesas

Range: westernmost quarter of Arizona

Notes: A common spring ephemeral of the Mojave Desert named for the five red spots found inside each bloom (see inset). It's also called Chinese lantern, as the flowers are globe-shaped with a small opening at the top and appear to glow when light shines through the delicate petals. The blossoms group together in the leaf junctions, opening in the afternoon and closing at night. The leaves of this short-lived, low-growing annual track the sun, turning to get the maximum amount of sunlight to make food (photosynthesis).

FLOWER TYPE	LEAF TYPE	LEAF ATTACHMENT	FRUIT
Regular	**Simple**	**Basal**	**Pod**

87

Rock Hibiscus
Hibiscus denudatus

Family: Mallow (Malvaceae)

Height: 12–24" (30–61 cm)

Flower: slightly cupped flowers of pale pink (can be white) to deep lavender, 1–1½" (2.5–4 cm) wide, have 5 slightly overlapping, broad wavy petals with pink-streaked bases around a pink center

Leaf: rounded triangular to oblong, grayish-green leaves, ½–1" (1–2.5 cm) long, are densely hairy with toothed edges; sparse and alternate along the several straggly stems

Fruit: 5-parted, star-shaped tan capsule with hairy seeds

Bloom: Jan–Oct, but nearly year-round after rain

Cycle/Origin: perennial; native

Zone/Habitat: desert scrub below 4,500' (1,370 m); rocky slopes, canyons, among creosote bushes, in sandy washes

Range: southern third of Arizona

Notes: Mallows are easily identified by the central column of fused male flower parts (stamens), which is usually some shade of red in rock hibiscus. The leaves are always sparse and sometimes missing altogether when the plant is flowering. It blooms following rain throughout most of the year. In its westernmost range, where it is called paleface, the flowers are white with red centers. Farther eastward, the blossoms are pink; they are purple in its easternmost range. The pink form grows in Saguaro National Park, near Tucson.

FLOWER TYPE	LEAF TYPE	LEAF ATTACHMENT	FRUIT
Regular	**Simple**	**Alternate**	**Pod**

New Mexico Checker Mallow
Sidalcea neomexicana

Family: Mallow (Malvaceae)

Height: 12–36" (30–91 cm)

Flower: deep-pink or purple blossoms, 1–1½" (2.5–4 cm) wide, in a loose spike cluster, 6–12" (15–30 cm) long; each bloom has 5 blunted broad petals veined with white and a green-and-white center

Leaf: fleshy fan-shaped basal leaves, 2–4" (5–10 cm) wide, on long stalks, have round-toothed edges; upper leaves are alternate and deeply divided into 5–6 irregular lobes

Bloom: Jun–Sep

Cycle/Origin: perennial; native

Zone/Habitat: riparian deciduous, montane, subalpine at 5,000–9,500' (1,525–2,895 m); meadows, along creeks, alkaline seeps and marshes, wet soils

Range: northern half of Arizona, except the northwestern corner; southeastern quarter of the state

Notes: Tolerant of salty water, this plant is also called salt spring checkerbloom. However, it frequently occurs near freshwater in Arizona, such as along Walnut Creek in the Apache-Sitgreaves National Forests in the east-central part of the state. Like others in the Mallow family, this flower's buds are twisted and flame-shaped, and the yellow flower parts are fused into a central column. The leaves have been cooked and eaten as greens by Indigenous Peoples.

CLUSTER TYPE
Spike

FLOWER TYPE
Regular

LEAF TYPE
Simple

LEAF TYPE
Simple Lobed

LEAF ATTACHMENT
Alternate

LEAF ATTACHMENT
Basal

fruit

Fairy Duster
Calliandra eriophylla

Family: Pea or Bean (Fabaceae)

Height: 12–36" (30–91 cm); shrub

Flower: round, fuzzy, pink-and-white cluster, 1–2" (2.5–5 cm) wide; each cluster consists mainly of long male flower parts (stamens) with yellow tips

Leaf: dark-green leaves, 1–1½" (2.5–4 cm) long, divided into 2–4 pairs of leaflets and again into 7–9 tiny oval subleaflets, bulbous gray stem; usually evergreen, but can drop leaves during cold or drought

Fruit: flat pea-like green pod, turning reddish brown, 2–4" (5–10 cm) long, is fuzzy with thickened edges; splits lengthwise with a loud popping sound, forcefully dispersing the seeds

Bloom: Oct–May

Cycle/Origin: perennial; native

Zone/Habitat: desert scrub, grasslands below 5,000' (1,525 m); flats, rocky slopes, along washes

Range: throughout, except the northeastern quarter

Notes: Thornless or with a few paired thorns on its stems, fairy duster is a low-growing branching shrub. When in bloom, it is covered with fluffy pink balls with yellow dots that appear to float above the surface of the flower. The flowers attract butterflies and hummingbirds; deer and javelinas (pig-like animals) eat the leaves. The curly open seedpods remain on the shrub for months.

CLUSTER TYPE
Round

FLOWER TYPE
Irregular

LEAF TYPE
Twice Compound

LEAF ATTACHMENT
Alternate

FRUIT
Pod

93

Feather Plume
Dalea formosa

Family: Pea or Bean (Fabaceae)

Height: 18–36" (45–91 cm); shrub

Flower: short, deep-violet-and-yellow spike cluster, 1–2" (2.5–5 cm) long, composed of 2–9 small pea-like purplish-pink flowers with the largest petal cream or yellow, surrounded by feathery sepals

Leaf: feather-like, grayish-green leaves, ¼–½" (.6–1 cm) long, made up of 7–15 tiny narrow leaflets; leaves are semi-evergreen

Bloom: Mar–Jun, especially after rainfall

Cycle/Origin: perennial; native

Zone/Habitat: desert scrub and grasslands at 2,000–6,500' (610–1,980 m); rocky hillsides, mountains

Range: eastern three-quarters of Arizona

Notes: Sometimes called feather dalea, this hardy, low-growing shrub is a good choice for cultivation in the Southwest. It tolerates cold and heat, and it blooms profusely with little water. Don't overwater—the plant will become leggy. It's pollinated by bees, but butterflies also visit the blossoms. Among the 36 species of prairie clover in Arizona, feather plume is the only one that forms a shrub with woody stems. It is especially common in the Chihuahuan Desert, part of which is located in southeastern Arizona, but feather plume is also found in New Mexico, Colorado, Utah, and northern Mexico.

CLUSTER TYPE
Spike

FLOWER TYPE
Irregular

LEAF TYPE
Compound

LEAF ATTACHMENT
Alternate

Colorado Four O'clock
Mirabilis multiflora

Family: Four O'clock (Nyctaginaceae)

Height: 16–27" (40–69 cm)

Flower: large, trumpet-shaped, purple-to-pink flowers, 1–3" (2.5–7.5 cm) long, centers sometimes dark, made up of fused petal-like sepals; held by papery cup of green bracts; in groups of 3–6 blooms

Leaf: short-stalked, round or oval leaves, 2–4" (5–10 cm) long, pointed or rounded tips, heart-shaped bases

Fruit: smooth or rough, oval brown pod, ½" (1 cm) long, sometimes with tan-and-brown ribs

Bloom: Apr–Sep

Cycle/Origin: perennial, native

Zone/Habitat: desert scrub, oak/pinyon pine/juniper woodlands and montane at 2,500–8,500' (760–2,590 m); open sandy areas, along roads, mesas

Range: throughout

Notes: *Mirabilis* means "wonderful" and *multiflora* is for "many flowers," referring to the multitude of spectacular blossoms on the mounded plants. The showy blooms open in late afternoon, emitting a musky fragrance nightly that attracts the hawk moth, its main pollinator. Hawk moths have a long snout or proboscis that can reach the nectar at the bottom of the funnel-shaped flower. The Navajo boiled the blooms, using the mixture to dye wool a light brown or purple. This plant is found throughout the Southwest.

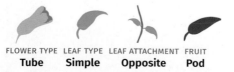

FLOWER TYPE **Tube** LEAF TYPE **Simple** LEAF ATTACHMENT **Opposite** FRUIT **Pod**

fruit

Arizona Rose
Rosa woodsii

Family: Rose (Rosaceae)

Height: 4–10' (1.2–3 m); shrub

Flower: groups of 2–5 light-pink flowers, 1½" (4 cm) wide, of 5 bluntly oval petals surrounding a bright-yellow center; backed by 5 narrowly pointed green sepals

Leaf: dark-green leaves, 2–5" (5–13 cm) long, divided into 5–11 oval leaflets, 1–2" (2.5–5 cm) long; toothed leaflets tipped with sticky glands; thorny stems

Fruit: hard, oval, berry-like green fruit, turning red when ripe, ½" (1 cm) wide

Bloom: May–Jul

Cycle/Origin: perennial; native

Zone/Habitat: riparian deciduous and montane at 4,000–9,000' (1,220–2,745 m); along streams, open areas in ponderosa pine forests, roadside ditches, moist soils

Range: northern half and southeastern quarter of Arizona

Notes: Arizona rose is the most widespread and abundant wild rose in the state. Its stout thorns, thick at the base and curving to a hooked point, resemble a cat's claws. The red fruits (called rose hips) contain large amounts of vitamin C and protein and can be made into jams, jellies, and wine. If you live in the mountains of Arizona, plant this rose to attract wildlife. The rose hips persist over winter and are a food source for wildlife. Elk and deer eat the leaves, and the older woody stems provide cover for birds and small animals.

FLOWER TYPE
Regular

LEAF TYPE
Compound

LEAF ATTACHMENT
Alternate

FRUIT
Berry

Fringed Twinevine
Funastrum cynanchoides

Family: Dogbane (Apocynaceae)

Height: 8–40' (2.4–12.2 m); vine

Flower: purplish-pink or white round cluster, 1½–4" (4–10 cm) wide, of 15–25 star-shaped flowers; each flower, ½" (1 cm) wide, has 5 pointed, fuzzy-edged, purplish-pink-and-white petals and 5 sepals around a white protruding center made up of 5 inflated sacs

Leaf: variable-shaped leaves, ½–2½" (1–6 cm) long, with pointed or rounded tips and blunt or lobed bases

Fruit: narrow purplish-green pod, turning brown, 1½–3½" (4–9 cm) long, is pointed at both ends, bulges in the middle, and contains reddish-brown seeds

Bloom: Apr–Oct

Cycle/Origin: perennial; native

Zone/Habitat: desert scrub and grasslands at 100–5,500' (30–1,675 m); on cacti, in ditches near cultivated fields

Range: throughout Arizona, except the northeastern corner

Notes: When broken or cut, the stems exude a white sap that smells foul and can irritate skin on contact. It grows from a large main root, which is hard to dig out; it will grow again from any small root piece left in the soil. Thus, although native, it can be an invasive weed in gardens and yards. The small seeds are attached to downy tufts that act as parachutes, which carry the seeds away on the wind, so it spreads readily from one area to another.

CLUSTER TYPE	FLOWER TYPE	LEAF TYPE	LEAF ATTACHMENT	FRUIT
Round	**Regular**	**Simple**	**Opposite**	**Pod**

Bird's Foot Morning Glory
Ipomoea ternifolia

Family: Morning Glory (Convolvulaceae)

Height: 12–36" (30–91 cm); vine

Flower: trumpet-shaped, purplish-pink flowers, 2" (5 cm) wide, made up of fused petals with darker pink bases, flaring widely around a white center; 1–2 blooms per stalk attached at a leaf junction (axis)

Leaf: hand-shaped leaves divided into 3–5 narrow lobes, 1–3" (2.5–7.5 cm) long, on stalks, alternate along the twining stem

Bloom: Jun–Oct

Cycle/Origin: annual; native

Zone/Habitat: desert scrub and grasslands at 2,500–4,500' (760–1,370 m); along washes, among grasses, in shrubs, flats, mesas

Range: southeastern quarter of Arizona

Notes: These showy, delicate-looking flowers don't appear until after the monsoon rains. The vines trail along the ground or twine in shrubs a few feet high. Blooms are sometimes pure white or purple, always opening in early morning and wilting by afternoon. Bird's foot can be mistaken for two other morning glory species that are not native to Arizona, tall morning glory (*Ipomoea purpurea*) (pg. 421) and ivyleaf morning glory (*I. hederacea*) (pg. 420). However, bird's foot has clearly thinner lobes to its leaves, resembling the three toes of a bird's foot, thus the common name. The two nonnative flowers are invasive and illegal to plant in Arizona.

FLOWER TYPE
Tube

LEAF TYPE
Simple Lobed

LEAF ATTACHMENT
Alternate

Arizona Valerian
Valeriana arizonica

Family: Honeysuckle (Caprifoliaceae)

Height: 8–14" (20–36 cm)

Flower: pale-pink-to-lavender blossoms in a spiky round cluster, 2" (5 cm) wide; each star-shaped, tubular flower, 1" (2.5 cm) long, has 5 petals around the darker pink throat and protruding pink or white male flower parts (stamens)

Leaf: spoon-shaped basal leaves, 2½–6½" (6–15 cm) long, are smooth and on long stalks; a few shorter arrow-shaped stem leaves have 2–3 pairs of lobes and clasp the hollow stems

Bloom: Apr–Jul

Cycle/Origin: perennial; native

Zone/Habitat: montane and subalpine at 4,500–8,000' (1,370–2,440 m); coniferous forests, moist rich soils

Range: northern half and southeastern quarter of Arizona

Notes: The pretty, frilly pink flowers of this mountain wildflower top the almost-leafless branching stems above the basal rosette of dark-green leaves. It is an attractive plant for moist places in the garden when planted at the correct elevation. The genus name *Valeriana* may be from the Latin word *valere*, which means "to be healthy and strong," referring to the use of these plants in folk medicine to treat anxiety.

CLUSTER TYPE
Round

FLOWER TYPE
Tube

LEAF TYPE
Simple

LEAF TYPE
Simple Lobed

LEAF ATTACHMENT
Opposite

LEAF ATTACHMENT
Basal

fruit

Showy Milkweed

Asclepias speciosa

Family: Milkweed (Asclepiadaceae)

Height: 1⅓–4' (40–129 cm)

Flower: Spherical, pink-and-white, fragrant clusters, 2–3" (5–8 cm) wide, of star-shaped pink flowers; each complex, crown-like bloom, 1" (2.5 cm) wide, has 5 upward-curving, light-pink horns and 5 dark-pink, downward-curving petals below

Leaf: wide, lance-like leaves, 3–8" (8–20 cm) long, with prominent central veins, smooth above, hairy below; in widely spaced pairs on straight stalks containing milky-white sap

Fruit: fuzzy, conical pod, 3–5" (7.6–13 cm) long, turns gray in fall, splits open, releasing brown seeds on silky plumes

Bloom: Jun–Aug

Cycle/Origin: perennial; native

Zone/Habitat: conifer woodlands, open meadows, moist areas, and roadsides, 5,000–9,000' (1,520–2,740 m)

Range: most of northern Arizona, except the state's northwest corner

Notes: Unlike most wildflowers, milkweed pollen is clumped in pairs of waxy sacs that resemble saddlebags. The pollen sacs catch on the legs of insects seeking nectar, which then carry these sticky bags away to other milkweed flowers. Poisonous milkweed leaves are necessary food for the caterpillars of monarch and queen butterflies, rendering them toxic to predators.

CLUSTER TYPE	FLOWER TYPE	LEAF TYPE	LEAF ATTACHMENT	FRUIT
Round	**Irregular**	**Simple**	**Opposite**	**Pod**

Grassleaf Pea
Lathyrus graminifolius

Family: Pea or Bean (Fabaceae)

Height: 12–30" (30–76 cm); vine

Flower: spike clusters, 2–3" (5–7.5 cm) long, of 4–6 typical pea flowers, ¾" (2 cm) wide; flowers are pink and white and bloom along 1 side of stalk

Leaf: alternately attached leaves, 2–3" (5–7.5 cm) long, divided into 3–4 opposite pairs of narrow grass-like leaflets, 2–3" (5–7.5 cm) long; each leaflet has a smooth margin; each end (terminal) leaflet is modified into a clinging forked tendril

Fruit: green pod, turning tan, 5" (13 cm) long, has a typical peapod shape

Bloom: May–Sep

Cycle/Origin: perennial; native

Zone/Habitat: grasslands and montane at 4,000–9,000' (1,220–2,745 m); forest clearings, slopes, gulches

Range: throughout Arizona, except the far western edge

Notes: The wild peas in this genus are weak-stemmed vines that climb up on other plants by taking hold with forked tendrils. Of the seven species of *Lathyrus* in Arizona, this has the narrowest grass-like blades, thus the name "grassleaf." Its blossoms resemble those of the common garden pea. Like other members of the Pea or Bean family, its roots fix nitrogen into the soil, improving soil fertility.

CLUSTER TYPE
Spike

FLOWER TYPE
Irregular

LEAF TYPE
Compound

LEAF ATTACHMENT
Alternate

FRUIT
Pod

109

Rocky Mountain Bee Plant
Cleome serrulata

Family: Spiderflower (Cleomaceae)

Height: 1–4' (30–122 cm)

Flower: dense, fuzzy-looking, purple or pink spike clusters, 2–3" (5–10 cm) long, made of dozens of small flowers; each blossom, ½" (1 cm) long, has 8 petals and petal-like sepals and long protruding flower parts

Leaf: lower leaves are dull green, long stalked, and divided into 3 oval leaflets, 1–3" (2.5–7.5 cm) long, with pointed tips and smooth or minutely toothed edges; simple leaves on upper part of waxy smooth stem

Fruit: curved bean-like green pod, 1–3" (2.5–7.5 cm) long, on a long stalk, turns brown, has 2 chambers containing several egg-shaped, mottled-brown seeds

Bloom: Jun–Sep

Cycle/Origin: annual; native

Zone/Habitat: desert scrub, grasslands, oak/pinyon pine/juniper woods, 4,500–7,000' (1,370–2,135 m); flats, slopes

Range: northern half of Arizona

Notes: This was a well-known plant to Navajo and other Native American tribes, who have used it in a variety of ways. The leaves have been cooked in meat stews or brewed into a tea to treat fevers and sore eyes. The seeds have been made into a mush or bread. A black paint has been made from the plant and has been used to decorate pottery.

CLUSTER TYPE
Spike

FLOWER TYPE
Regular

LEAF TYPE
Simple

LEAF TYPE
Compound

LEAF ATTACHMENT
Alternate

FRUIT
Pod

111

New Mexico Thistle

Cirsium neomexicanum

Family: Aster (Asteraceae)

Height: 2–10' (0.6–3 m)

Flower: pink-to-pale-lavender flower head, 2–3" (5–7.5 cm) wide, disk-shaped, of thin tubular disk flowers on a spherical green base of spiny bracts that narrows near its top; outer bracts pointing downward

Leaf: oblong leaves, 2½–14" (6–36 cm) long, dark green, each lobe ending in a sharp spine, stalkless or with winged leafstalks; upper stem leaves are much smaller, clasping; stem branches above the middle

Bloom: Mar–Jul

Cycle/Origin: perennial, biennial; native

Zone/Habitat: desert scrub, grasslands, and pinyon pine/juniper woodlands at 1,000–6,500' (305–1,980 m); slopes, plains, mesas, roadsides, canyons

Range: throughout

Notes: Colorful and often noticed along highways in Arizona, this is possibly the most common and widespread of the 17 species of thistle in the state. The usually pink or purple flowers can be white on some plants. Thistles are generally disliked for their spines and tendency to invade pastures (cattle avoid the plant). However, thistles are a good resource for wildlife. Hummingbirds and butterflies love the nectar. The seeds are a favorite food of the lesser goldfinch, which raises its young in late summer. This bird lines its nest with the thistledown produced after the thistles flower.

FLOWER TYPE
Composite

LEAF TYPE
Simple Lobed

LEAF ATTACHMENT
Alternate

LEAF ATTACHMENT
Clasping

113

Bush Penstemon
Penstemon ambiguus

Family: Plantain (Plantaginaceae)

Height: 12–16" (30–40 cm)

Flower: loose clusters of funnel-shaped blooms of pastel pink to white, 2–6" (6–15 cm) long; 1" (2.5 cm) wide, with 5 petals bent backward presenting a pansy-like face, throat of blossom lined with purplish-pink, hairy nectar guidelines

Leaf: bright-green, threadlike leaves, ⅕–1" (5–30 mm) long, taper to a point and attach directly to the multiple thin stems in opposite pairs

Fruit: teardrop-shaped, brown capsules, ⅓" (9 mm) long, split open with many tiny dark-brown seeds

Bloom: May–Oct

Cycle/Origin: perennial; native

Zone/Habitat: sandy soils, short grass grasslands, creosote and sagebrush deserts, pine-juniper woodlands at 4,500–6,500' (1,372–1,981 m)

Range: densely occurs in north-central and northeastern Arizona; sporadically near Tucson

Notes: Bush penstemon forms a mounded bush of multiple thin stems with a woody base. The lobes of the abundant blossoms flatten outward, covering the shrub in clouds of light pink, unlike the characteristic sparse-flowered look of other penstemons in Arizona. With appropriate rainfall, it produces spectacular flower shows turning dunes, mesas, and hillsides bright pink and white.

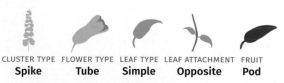

CLUSTER TYPE
Spike

FLOWER TYPE
Tube

LEAF TYPE
Simple

LEAF ATTACHMENT
Opposite

FRUIT
Pod

115

Scarlet Beeblossom
Gaura coccinea

Family: Evening-primrose (Onagraceae)

Height: 8–24" (20–61 cm)

Flower: spike cluster, 2–16" (5–40 cm) long, of flowers that turn overnight from white to pink to red; each blossom has 4 clawed petals and dangling red-tipped white male flower parts (anthers) backed by 4 downward-curving pointed pinkish-green sepals

Leaf: narrow, lance-shaped, grayish-green leaves, ½–3" (1–7.5 cm) long, have pointed tips and irregularly toothed or smooth edges; upper leaves smaller; several stems branching from base

Fruit: wrinkled diamond-shaped fruit, ½" (1 cm) long

Bloom: Apr–Sep

Cycle/Origin: perennial; native

Zone/Habitat: all life zones except subalpine at 2,000–8,000' (610–2,440 m); disturbed areas, among pines, old fields

Range: throughout, except the southwestern corner

Notes: This pretty, airy flower starts out almost white in the evening when it first opens, attracting moths that pollinate it. It turns pink by morning and red by afternoon. Flowers at the bottom of the spike open first. It spreads by underground stems, forming masses of plants, and it can colonize in heavily grazed or disturbed sites in regions outside of its natural range. The Navajo have produced a tea from this plant to help treat stomach upset.

CLUSTER TYPE
Spike

FLOWER TYPE
Irregular

LEAF TYPE
Simple

LEAF ATTACHMENT
Alternate

FRUIT
Pod

Pink Coralbells
Heuchera rubescens

Family: Saxifrage (Saxifragaceae)

Height: 5–12" (13–30 cm)

Flower: light-pink spike clusters, 3–20" (7.5–50 cm) long, with many groups of vase-shaped flowers angling from thin stalks along a slender fuzzy stalk; each tiny blossom has 5 sticky, hairy, green-tipped sepals forming a vase holding 5 longer downward curving petals and protruding flower parts

Leaf: long-stalked round basal leaves, ½–1½" (1–4 cm) wide, with 5–9 shallow-toothed lobes; teeth are tipped with bristles

Bloom: May–Oct

Cycle/Origin: perennial; native

Zone/Habitat: montane and subalpine at 6,500–11,500' (1,980–3,510 m); dry-to-moist soils near shaded rocks, along rocky streams, coniferous forests

Range: northern half and southeastern corner of Arizona

Notes: The family name Saxifrage is from Latin words for "rock" and "break," referring to the habit of growing in rock outcroppings. This pretty, delicate flower makes an attractive addition to rock gardens in cool climates. The root contains alum, a drying agent that has been used to stop diarrhea, thus another name for this widespread species is pink alumroot. Limited to the southeastern corner of Arizona, the similar coralbells (pg. 123) has larger, dark-pink-to-red, bell-shaped flowers with flower parts that don't stick out.

CLUSTER TYPE
Spike

FLOWER TYPE
Tube

LEAF TYPE
Simple Lobed

LEAF ATTACHMENT
Basal

Arizona Milkvetch

Astragalus arizonicus

Family: Pea or Bean (Fabaceae)

Height: 6–20" (15–50 cm)

Flower: purplish-pink, pea-like flowers in spike clusters, 4–6" (10–15 cm) long; each bloom, ½" (1 cm) long, has an erect, purplish-pink upper petal (banner) with a large white spot with purplish-pink veins

Leaf: feather-like, grayish-green leaves, 1–4" (2.5–10 cm) long, are alternate and divided into 2–8 pairs of hairy, narrow pointed leaflets

Fruit: erect tan pod, ½–1" (1–2.5 cm) long, is slender and flat; splits into 2 parts down the center

Bloom: Mar–May

Cycle/Origin: perennial; native

Zone/Habitat: desert scrub and grasslands at 2,500–4,500' (760–1,370 m); along roads, flats, mesas, rocky soils

Range: two-thirds of Arizona, in a wide band from the northwestern to southeastern parts of the state

Notes: This member of the Pea or Bean family has radiating, sprawling stems with erect flower spikes of relatively large, pea-like blossoms. The spikes rise above the silky-haired, grayish-green foliage. It's common in disturbed areas and in rocky soils throughout most of Arizona. It also occurs in New Mexico and northern Mexico. This plant is reported to have poisoned cattle, thus it has another common name, Arizona locoweed.

CLUSTER TYPE
Spike

FLOWER TYPE
Irregular

LEAF TYPE
Compound

LEAF ATTACHMENT
Alternate

FRUIT
Pod

Coralbells

Heuchera sanguinea

Family: Saxifrage (Saxifragaceae)

Height: 12–24" (30–61 cm)

Flower: loose, dark-pink-to-coral-red clusters, 4–6" (10–15 cm) long, of bell-shaped flowers, dangling from thin stalks widely spaced along a slender fuzzy red stalk; each small blossom, ½" (1 cm) long, has 5 pointed petals around short yellow flower parts

Leaf: rounded heart-shaped basal leaves, 3" (7.5 cm) wide, are mottled cream on green, have toothed lobes, and are on long stalks

Bloom: Mar–Oct

Cycle/Origin: perennial; native

Zone/Habitat: riparian deciduous, montane, subalpine at 4,000–8,500' (1,220–2,590 m); moist soils near shaded rocks, along rocky streams, coniferous forests

Range: southeastern corner of Arizona

Notes: This showy wildflower is only found in the southeastern corner of Arizona, in a small area of southwestern New Mexico, and in northern Mexico. It has dark-pink-to-red, bell-shaped flowers with flower parts that do not stick out, unlike the similar-but-paler pink coralbells (pg. 119), which has tiny, light-pink, vase-shaped flowers with protruding flower parts. Coralbells forms a low mound, with flowers on stalks well above the foliage. It is often grown as a ground cover for its marbled cream-and-green leaves and for its attractive blooms.

CLUSTER TYPE	FLOWER TYPE	LEAF TYPE	LEAF ATTACHMENT
Spike	**Bell**	**Simple Lobed**	**Basal**

Desert Penstemon
Penstemon pseudospectabilis

Family: Plantain (Plantaginaceae)

Height: 1–4' (30–122 cm)

Flower: funnel-shaped, drooping, bright-rosy-pink flowers, ¾" (2 cm) long, in open spike clusters, 6–24" (15–61 cm) long; each sticky hairy bloom has a bulge in lower half of tube, 3 rounded lower lobes bent downward, flat upper half with 2 rounded upright lobes; bearded, protruding, fifth male flower part

Leaf: stalkless, triangular, glossy leaves, 1–3½" (2.5–9 cm) long, toothed edges turned upward, fused together at their bases around smooth purplish-green stems

Fruit: oval brown capsules, ½" (1 cm) long, held by persistent cup-shaped bracts on short stalks

Bloom: Feb–May

Cycle/Origin: perennial; native

Zone/Habitat: desert scrub, oak/pinyon pine/juniper woodlands at 2,500–7,000' (760–2,135 m); canyons, washes

Range: throughout

Notes: It's similar in appearance to parry penstemon (pg. 127), but desert penstemon has darker pink and broader tubular flowers, as well as wider triangular leaves. It's often cultivated in gardens, as it attracts hummingbirds. There are nearly 40 species of penstemon in Arizona; hummingbirds and bumblebees are the two major pollinators of these wildflowers.

CLUSTER TYPE	FLOWER TYPE	LEAF TYPE	LEAF ATTACHMENT	LEAF ATTACHMENT	FRUIT
Spike	**Tube**	**Simple**	**Opposite**	**Perfoliate**	**Pod**

Parry Penstemon

Penstemon parryi

Family: Plantain (Plantaginaceae)

Height: 1½–4' (45–122 cm)

Flower: open spike cluster, 12–36" (30–91 cm) long, of pink tubular flowers; each flower, ½–¾" (1–2 cm) long, has fused petals forming a tube, flaring at the mouth; rounded 2-lobed upper and 3-lobed lower petals with darker pink middle vein; flowers in whorls about the almost-leafless upper stem

Leaf: narrowly elliptical or spoon-shaped, bluish-green leaves, 1½–6" (4–15 cm) long, are fleshy and stalk-less, with smooth edges curling slightly upward; upper leaves much smaller

Bloom: Mar–Apr

Cycle/Origin: perennial; native

Zone/Habitat: desert scrub at 800–5,000' (245–1,525 m); canyons, flats, slopes, along washes

Range: southeastern Arizona and the area near Phoenix, often planted along highways and on medians

Notes: This pretty pink wildflower occurs only in Arizona in the US, but it is very common at the lower elevations within its life zone. The seeds are a food source for birds such as Gambel's quail. It's a favorite plant for desert landscaping and for butterfly and hummingbird gardens, as hummingbirds drink the nectar and pollinate the blooms. It's often cultivated, growing readily from seed. Desert cottontails eat the seedlings, so the young plants must be protected.

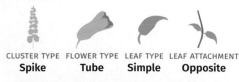

CLUSTER TYPE	FLOWER TYPE	LEAF TYPE	LEAF ATTACHMENT
Spike	**Tube**	**Simple**	**Opposite**

leaves

Palmer Penstemon
Penstemon palmeri

Family: Plantain (Plantaginaceae)

Height: 5–6' (1.5–1.8 m)

Flower: fragrant, large-mouthed, pale-pink-to-lilac flowers, 1½" (4 cm) long, in an open or dense spike cluster, 3' (0.9 m) long; each balloon-like bloom has 2 lobes flaring backward and 3 lobes bending downward; lobes are streaked with magenta

Leaf: triangular leathery leaves, 1–5" (2.5–13 cm) long, edges toothed or wavy, curving upward; smaller upper leaves joined at bases surrounding tall stems

Fruit: erect cup-shaped tan capsules, ½" (1 cm) long

Bloom: Mar–Sep

Cycle/Origin: perennial; native

Zone/Habitat: desert scrub, oak/pinyon pine/juniper woods and montane at 3,500–6,500' (1,065–1,980 m); along washes, slopes, among sagebrush, canyon floors

Range: northern half of Arizona, except the northeastern corner of the state

Notes: The tallest penstemon in the Southwest, it has showy, honey-scented blooms. A member of a group of penstemons with flowers designed for bee pollination, it provides a landing platform and a swollen tube to accommodate the chubby bodies of bumblebees. The other group has narrow tubular red flowers that fit the needle-like bills of hummingbirds.

CLUSTER TYPE
Spike

FLOWER TYPE
Tube

LEAF TYPE
Simple

LEAF ATTACHMENT
Opposite

LEAF ATTACHMENT
Perfoliate

FRUIT
Pod

Small-flowered Milkvetch
Astragalus nuttallianus

Family: Pea or Bean (Fabaceae)

Height: 6–12" (15–30 cm)

Flower: small pea-like purple flower, ¼–½" (0.6–1 cm) long, has an erect purple-to-blue upper petal (banner) with a large purple-veined white spot; 1–7 blooms grouped at end of the stems

Leaf: bright-green feather-like leaves, 3" (7.5 cm) long, divided into 7–15 white-haired, narrowly oval leaflets; erect or trailing reddish stems

Fruit: smooth or hairy, curved slender pods, 1" (2.5 cm) long, are green and turn reddish when mature; pods are horizontal from the stem tips

Bloom: Feb–May

Cycle/Origin: annual; native

Zone/Habitat: desert scrub, grasslands, oak/pinyon pine/juniper woods at 100–4,000' (30–1,220 m); flats, mesas

Range: throughout

Notes: It's the most common of the annual milkvetch species in Arizona. Variable, it can grow in mats of sprawling stems sometimes less than an inch high or have erect stems up to a foot tall. Flower color also varies from white to light or neon blue, or from pink to purple. It can have smooth or hairy pods. It ranges from California east to Oklahoma and south to Mexico. Toxic to livestock, it can cause loss of weight, inability to control the hind legs, or total paralysis.

FLOWER TYPE	LEAF TYPE	LEAF ATTACHMENT	FRUIT
Irregular	**Compound**	**Alternate**	**Pod**

bristly leaves

Bristly Nama
Nama hispida

Family: Forget-me-not (Boraginaceae)

Height: 3–12" (7.5–30 cm)

Flower: upright tube flower, ½" (1 cm) wide, appears as a regular flower from above but is actually tubular with 5 rounded spreading lobes; blooms are purple to reddish pink to a pink-and-white combination, each with a pale-yellow throat

Leaf: long and narrow to spoon-shaped leaves, ½–2" (1–5 cm) long, are grayish green, sticky, hairy, with blunt tips; the edges are partially rolled under; ends of sprawling, branching stems grow erectly

Bloom: Feb–Jun

Cycle/Origin: annual; native

Zone/Habitat: desert scrub below 5,000' (1,525 m); flats

Range: eastern two-thirds of Arizona

Notes: Bristly Nama is extremely common and abundant, forming mats that can carpet large areas of desert after heavy winter rains. In drought years, only a few plants producing a handful of flowers grow along washes, where some moisture is still available below the surface. This species is sometimes called sandbells due to its preference for sandy soils and for the tubular flowers with widely spreading lobes, resembling upright bells. When cultivated and with added water, it makes a good, low-growing ground cover that blooms profusely throughout the summer.

FLOWER TYPE   LEAF TYPE   LEAF ATTACHMENT
Tube   **Simple**   **Alternate**

fruit

Snapdragonvine
Maurandella antirrhiniflora

Family: Plantain (Plantaginaceae)

Height: 3–10' (.9–3 m); vine

Flower: snapdragon-like purple flower, ½–¾" (1–2 cm) long, has 2 upper erect lobes, 3 lower lobes, a triangular swollen white throat with a hairy bump lined with purple, and a spotted tube; 5 pointed green sepals

Leaf: broad arrowhead-shaped leaves, ½–2" (1–5 cm) long, are dark-to-bright green, on a twining stem

Fruit: round green pod, ⅓" (.8 cm) wide, turning reddish brown, has a thread-like stem in middle; pod held by 5 pointed, persistent sepals that flare outward

Bloom: Mar–Sep

Cycle/Origin: perennial; native

Zone/Habitat: desert scrub, oak/pinyon pine/juniper woodlands at 1,500–6,000' (460–1,830 m); flats, slopes

Range: throughout Arizona, except the northeastern corner of the state

Notes: This delicate-looking vine is often cultivated in Arizona for its showy, small flowers, which can be blue or reddish pink. Snapdragonvine has ivy-like leaves and grows well when planted in a pot with a trellis. A food plant for common buckeye butterfly caterpillars, it is often planted in butterfly gardens. It's usually deciduous, dying off in winter and growing from the root in spring. However, it is semi-evergreen in some protected habitats.

FLOWER TYPE   LEAF TYPE   LEAF ATTACHMENT   FRUIT
Tube   **Simple**   **Alternate**   **Pod**

135

Wanderer Violet
Viola nephrophylla

Family: Violet (Violaceae)

Height: 2–12" (5–30 cm)

Flower: unusual nodding, deep-violet flower, ½–1" (1–2.5 cm) long, has 5 petals with distinct blue or darker purple veins; 2 erect upper petals and 3 lower bearded petals have white bases; middle lower petal has a short sac-like spur

Leaf: wide, heart- or kidney-shaped basal leaves, 1–2½" (2.5–6 cm) long, are dark green above and purplish green below; round-toothed edges; on long stalks

Fruit: 3-valved elliptical capsule, ¼–½" (0.6–1 cm) long

Bloom: Apr–Jul

Cycle/Origin: annual, perennial; native

Zone/Habitat: riparian deciduous, montane, subalpine at 5,000–9,500' (1,525–2,895 m); moist meadows, canyons, seeps, mountain slopes, along streams

Range: eastern two-thirds of Arizona

Notes: A stemless, low-growing violet, its smooth leafstalks and leafless flower stalks arise directly from underground stems. Early settlers made a jelly from the flowers and a tea that was used to treat headaches and sore throats. The leaves are very high in vitamins A and C. Because it grows only in moist places, it is often called northern bog violet. Widespread throughout the United States, except for the southeastern states, it's also found in the boreal forests of Canada.

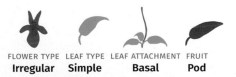

FLOWER TYPE	LEAF TYPE	LEAF ATTACHMENT	FRUIT
Irregular	**Simple**	**Basal**	**Pod**

Chaparral Nightshade
Solanum xanti

Family: Nightshade (Solanaceae)

Height: 16–36" (40–91 cm)

Flower: loose groups of 4–9 dark-purple, star-shaped flowers, on short slender flower stalks; each radially symmetrical blossom, ½–1" (1.5–2.5 cm) wide, has 5 triangular, very wrinkled, papery petals fused around bright-yellow protruding flower parts

Leaf: dark-green leaves, oval to lance shaped, ¾–3" (2–4 cm) long, with wavy edges; alternate on fuzzy, branching green stalks

Fruit: round, green berry, ½" (1.3 cm) wide, has smooth skin and dangles in loose groups from stalks

Bloom: Apr–Nov

Cycle/Origin: perennial; native

Zone/Habitat: rocky, bajada slopes in chaparral, 3,500–5,500' (1,070–1,680 m)

Range: northwestern and north-central, occurring in about two-thirds of Arizona

Notes: The species name *xanti* is in honor of Janos Xantus (1825–1894), a Hungarian natural history collector who worked extensively in the United States and Mexico and for whom many plants, birds, and animals are named. Although silverleaf and chaparral nightshade flowers are very alike, the orange spines on the gray stems of silverleaf (p. 143) separate it from chaparral, which has slightly fuzzy green stems. All parts of this plant are toxic and thus avoided by deer.

FLOWER TYPE **Regular** LEAF TYPE **Simple** LEAF ATTACHMENT **Alternate** FRUIT **Berry**

Brown-plumed Wire Lettuce
Stephanomeria pauciflora

Family: Aster (Asteraceae)

Height: 8–20" (20–50 cm); shrub

Flower: pale-lavender-to-pink flower head, ¾" (2 cm) wide, with 5 strap-like petals (ray flowers) with 4 notches at the tips around 5 lavender-and-white male flower parts (stamens)

Leaf: basal, narrowly lance-shaped, bluish-green leaves, 1–3" (2.5–7.5 cm) long, with a white midrib and sharp lobes; basal leaves wither before the plant flowers; narrow unlobed stem leaves are tiny; up to 5 wiry, bluish-green, multibranching stems

Bloom: year-round

Cycle/Origin: perennial; native

Zone/Habitat: desert scrub, grasslands, oak/pinyon pine/juniper woods at 150–7,000' (50–2,135 m); along canyon walls, flats, slopes, along washes

Range: throughout Arizona, except the southwestern corner of the state

Notes: The basal rosette of this common aster dies before the plant blooms, and the twisting and branching stems form an open rounded shrub with few flowers, thus the plant is often overlooked. It's named "brown-plumed" for the feathery brown bristles on its fruit. "Wire" refers to the wiry, almost leafless, bluish-green stems. The blooms of the other seven species of wire lettuce in Arizona have more petals.

FLOWER TYPE
Regular

LEAF TYPE
Simple

LEAF TYPE
Simple Lobed

LEAF ATTACHMENT
Alternate

LEAF ATTACHMENT
Basal

fruit

Silverleaf Nightshade
Solanum elaeagnifolium

Family: Nightshade (Solanaceae)

Height: 1–4' (30–122 cm)

Flower: loose groups of star-shaped purple (sometimes white) flowers; each flower, ¾–1½" (2–4 cm) wide, has 5 long triangular fused petals that are wrinkled and thin with wavy edges and surround the bright-yellow protruding flower parts

Leaf: narrowly lance-shaped, greenish-gray leaves, 1–6" (2.5–15 cm) long, with wavy margins and orange spines on veins below; long straight thorns on stems

Fruit: round berry-like fruit, ⅓–⅔" (0.8–1.6 cm) wide, is smooth and hard; mottled green, turning orangish yellow when ripe; dangles from thorny stalk

Bloom: May–Oct

Cycle/Origin: perennial; native

Zone/Habitat: desert scrub and grasslands at 1,000–5,000' (305–1,525 m); abandoned fields, disturbed soils

Range: throughout

Notes: The grayish cast to the stems and leaves is from the covering of dense, star-shaped hairs. An invasive weed toxic to livestock, it spreads by deep underground stems, forming colonies that are hard to eradicate. The plant, which contains a digestive enzyme, has been combined with animal brain tissue and used to tan hides. Pima People have used the crushed fruit to curdle milk when making cheese.

FLOWER TYPE
Regular

LEAF TYPE
Simple

LEAF ATTACHMENT
Alternate

FRUIT
Berry

Wild Mint
Mentha arvensis

Family: Mint (Lamiaceae)

Height: 6–24" (15–61 cm)

Flower: open round cluster, 1" (2.5 cm) wide, of small flowers of pale lilac or white; each flower, ¼" (0.6 cm) long; flower cluster encircles the square stem where each pair of leaves attaches

Leaf: pairs of lance-shaped leaves, 1–2" (2.5–5 cm) long, tapering at both ends, toothed margins; leaves get smaller near the top of plant; leaves have a strong odor when crushed

Bloom: Jul–Oct

Cycle/Origin: perennial; native

Zone/Habitat: oak/pinyon pine/juniper woods, riparian deciduous and montane at 5,000–9,000' (1,525–2,745 m); moist forests, along streams and lakes

Range: northeastern two-thirds of Arizona and scattered locations in southern half of the state

Notes: Native to Arizona, and the only native mint in *Mentha* (genus of the so-called "true mints") in the United States, it's sometimes called American wild mint. One way plants eliminate waste is by sequestering byproduct chemicals in their leaves in the form of essential oils. These oils, which give the leaves of this plant a minty smell and taste, have been used as flavoring in beverages and other foods.

CLUSTER TYPE
Round

FLOWER TYPE
Irregular

LEAF TYPE
Simple

LEAF ATTACHMENT
Opposite

centrally
striped, bell
flower

Arizona Phacelia
Phacelia arizonica

Family: Waterleaf (Hydrophyllaceae)

Height: 2–16" (5–40 cm)

Flower: tightly coiled, spike cluster, 1" (2.5 cm) long, of many bell-shaped, white or lavender flowers; each upright flower, ¼–½" (.6–1 cm) wide, has 5 rounded petals with a central pink stripe, and the flower parts protrude

Leaf: mostly basal, fern-like leaves, 1–3" (3–8 cm) long, very few shorter stem leaves alternately attached; overall oblong in shape, divided once or twice into pairs of finely hairy, toothed leaflets; purplish-green stems are sticky, hairy, and prostrate or upright

Bloom: Feb–May

Cycle/Origin: annual, perennial; native

Zone/Habitat: dry sunny areas on rocky hillsides or mesas in deserts or grasslands at 1,500–5,000' (457–1,524 m)

Range: southern half of Arizona, except the southwestern corner of the state

Notes: Arizona phacelia is found only in southern Arizona, southwestern New Mexico, and northern Mexico. Like other phacelias, the densely flowered spike is coiled like a scorpion's tail, thus it can be called Arizona scorpionweed. Unlike most other phacelias, however, Arizona phacelia has distinctively basal, deeply divided leaves; shorter blooming spikes; and centrally striped petals. It only blooms when winter rains have been plentiful.

CLUSTER TYPE
Spike

FLOWER TYPE
Bell

LEAF TYPE
Compound

LEAF TYPE
Twice Compound

LEAF ATTACHMENT
Basal

scorpiod
inflorescence

Blue Phacelia
Phacelia distans

Family: Forget-me-not (Boraginaceae)

Height: 6–32" (15–80 cm); shrub

Flower: tightly coiled, hairy spike cluster, 1" (2.5 cm) long, of many bell-shaped, bluish-purple flowers; each flower, ¼–½" (0.6–1 cm) wide, has 5 rounded petals around a bluish-purple center; flowers turn blue when wilted

Leaf: fern-like leaves, 1–4" (2.5–10 cm) long, are broadly lance-shaped, alternately attached, and divided once or twice into pairs of finely hairy, toothed leaflets; branching reddish stem has sparse stiff hairs

Bloom: Feb–May

Cycle/Origin: annual, perennial; native

Zone/Habitat: desert scrub and interior chaparral at 1,000–4,000' (305–1,220 m); along washes, flats, rocky slopes

Range: throughout, except the northeastern corner

Notes: It's also called scorpionweed for the spike, which resembles the coiled segmented tail of a scorpion. However, the scorpion's tail curls upward, while the flower spike curls downward. The flowers vary in color from purple to blue to white and bloom from the bottom up on the spike. Although the more than 30 species of phacelia in Arizona are hard to distinguish from each other, this one is easily identified by its pale-purple flowers, weak straggly stems, and its habit of growing under and getting tangled in other bushes.

CLUSTER TYPE
Spike

FLOWER TYPE
Regular

LEAF TYPE
Compound

LEAF TYPE
Twice Compound

LEAF ATTACHMENT
Alternate

Wild Hyacinth
Dichelostemma capitatum

Family: Lily (Liliaceae)

Height: 6–30" (15–76 cm)

Flower: loose group of 2–15 flowers atop a leafless stalk; each funnel-shaped flower, 1" (2.5 cm) wide, is bluish or pinkish purple and has 6 partially fused petals with pointed lobes flaring outward

Leaf: basal leaves, 4–27½" (10–70 cm) long, are narrow and grass-like; only 2–3 leaves rise from the bulb; leaves often dry up before the plant flowers

Bloom: Feb–May

Cycle/Origin: perennial; native

Zone/Habitat: desert scrub, grasslands, oak woodlands, montane below 7,000' (2,135 m); flats, rocky slopes

Range: two-thirds of Arizona, in a wide band from the northwestern to southeastern parts of the state

Notes: The species name *capitatum* means "head-like," referring to the group of flowers that tops the leafless, fleshy flower stalk. The number of flowers in the group varies from 2–5 (sometimes as many as 15), depending on the variety. Often found blooming abundantly in areas cleared by fire, it thrives due to the increased nutrients in the soil. Indigenous Peoples have dug up the bulbs, which taste similar to new potatoes, eating them raw or cooked. Wild hyacinth grows only in the western United States, ranging north to Oregon and east to New Mexico.

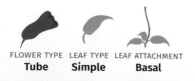

FLOWER TYPE
Tube

LEAF TYPE
Simple

LEAF ATTACHMENT
Basal

Trailing Four O'clock
Allionia incarnata

Family: Four O'clock (Nyctaginaceae)

Height: 1–5' (30–152 cm); vine

Flower: appears to be a regular flower, 1" (2.5 cm) wide, composed of 9 flat, 2-lobed, pinkish-purple petals surrounding a magenta-and-yellow center, but it is actually made up of 3 irregular flowers on a short stalk growing from a leaf attachment

Leaf: oval leaves, ¾–3" (2–7.5 cm) long, dull green above and gray below, blunt bases, usually pointed tips, edges smooth or wavy; pairs of leaves of unequal size; sticky, hairy stem

Bloom: Mar–Oct, in almost any season after rainfall

Cycle/Origin: annual, perennial; native

Zone/Habitat: desert scrub, grasslands below 6,000' (1,830 m); along roads and washes, slopes, mesas

Range: throughout

Notes: This ground-hugging vine has what appears to be one regular round flat flower, but it actually has three irregular flowers that bloom at the same time. It blooms after rain in all but the coldest weather. It occurs wherever there is sandy soil, often in disturbed areas. The sticky, hairy leaves are usually dotted with sand. Indigenous Peoples have used this plant to treat swelling and fever, brewing it into a tea to treat diarrhea or kidney disease. It occurs throughout the Southwest.

FLOWER TYPE **Irregular**   LEAF TYPE **Simple**   LEAF ATTACHMENT **Opposite**

153

Pleated Gentian
Gentiana affinis

Family: Gentian (Gentianaceae)

Height: 4–16" (10–40 cm)

Flower: 5–10 urn-shaped, violet-to-bluish-purple flowers, 1–1½" (2.5–4 cm) long, crowded at top of stalk; each bloom is held by long pointed green bracts, has 5 petals that are dull bluish purple below and joined by a membrane between each petal

Leaf: rough leaves, lance shaped to elliptical, ½–1½" (1–4 cm) long; pairs of leaves evenly spaced along erect or sprawling, burgundy-colored stems; the middle pairs are the longest

Bloom: Aug–Oct

Cycle/Origin: perennial; native

Zone/Habitat: montane and subalpine at 7,500–9,500' (2,285–2,895 m); meadows, along streams and springs, damp soils

Range: eastern half of Arizona

Notes: The genus *Gentiana* is named for King Gentius of ancient Illyria. "Pleated" in the common name is for the inward-folding membrane that joins the petals. It grows scattered in dense clusters of as many as a dozen plants in wet meadows and is sometimes called marsh gentian. Cultivated in rock gardens with damp areas where the sprawling stems can dangle over and be supported by stones, this wildflower can be seen on the famous Mount Baldy Trail in the White Mountains of east-central Arizona.

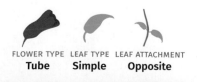

FLOWER TYPE   LEAF TYPE   LEAF ATTACHMENT
Tube   **Simple**   **Opposite**

Tansyleaf Tansy-aster

Machaeranthera tanacetifolia

Family: Aster (Asteraceae)

Height: 4–20" (10–50 cm)

Flower: bluish-violet flower head, 1–2" (2.5–5 cm) wide, is daisy-like and has 12–40 narrow petals (ray flowers) surrounding a yellow center (disk flowers)

Leaf: oval feathery leaves, ⅓–4½" (0.8–11 cm) long, are grayish green, alternately attached, sticky, hairy, and highly divided into opposite pairs of lobes; each lobe is tipped with bristly hairs; reddish-green stems are also hairy

Bloom: Jun–Oct

Cycle/Origin: annual, biennial; native

Zone/Habitat: desert scrub, oak/pinyon pine/juniper woodlands at 1,000–7,000' (305–2,135 m); along streams or roads, among creosote bushes, in old fields or disturbed areas

Range: throughout, except the southwestern corner

Notes: There are 13 species of tansy-asters in the *Machaeranthera* genus in Arizona; most are recognizable by the spiny bristle at the tip of each leaf lobe. The Greek words *machaer* and *anthera* in the genus name refer to the sword shape of the tips of the male flower parts (anthers). This tansy-aster can be identified by its fern-like or feathery leaves. It is sometimes cultivated from seed for its many showy flowers.

FLOWER TYPE
Composite

LEAF TYPE
Simple Lobed

LEAF ATTACHMENT
Alternate

Hoary Tansy-aster
Machaeranthera (Dieteria) asteroides

Family: Aster (Asteraceae)

Height: 2–4' (61–122 cm)

Flower: daisy-like, pinkish-lavender flower head, 1–2" (2.5–5 cm) wide, has many narrow, blunt-tipped petals surrounding a yellow center; 4–8 overlapping rows of pointed sticky bracts, pale greenish white with green tips, curving outward

Leaf: narrow basal leaves, 1–4" (2.5–10 cm) long, with smooth margins; alternating stem leaves (cauline) are broader; upper stem leaves gradually reduced to tiny bracts; 1 to many stems are multibranched

Bloom: Jun–Nov

Cycle/Origin: annual, perennial, biennial; native

Zone/Habitat: all life zones at 100–9,000' (30–2,745 m); disturbed ground, along roads and washes, riverbanks

Range: northern half of Arizona; the southernmost quarter, especially along the Santa Cruz River in Tucson

Notes: It's a highly variable aster, growing in many habitats and at most elevations in Arizona. This is a sprawling or erect plant with many branches and widely spaced leaves. It can have just a few scattered groups of flowers to many dense blooms topping the stems. Aptly named, "hoary" is for the sometimes pale-gray appearance of the velvety stems, and the species name *canescens* is Latin for "becoming gray." The seed heads are tan, fluffy, and dandelion-like.

FLOWER TYPE	LEAF TYPE	LEAF ATTACHMENT	LEAF ATTACHMENT
Composite	**Simple**	**Alternate**	**Basal**

Nodding Onion
Allium cernuum

Family: Amaryllis (Amaryllidaceae)

Height: 4–20" (10–50 cm)

Flower: drooping round cluster, 1–2" (2.5–5 cm) wide, of 8–35 bell-shaped lilac flowers (light pink or white when first open), whorled at the tip of the leafless flower stalk, which is bent like a shepherd's crook

Leaf: 3–5 grass-like leaves, 4–10" (10–25 cm) long, grow from the base of the plant and are flat or have a V-shaped channel

Fruit: 3-celled capsules held in nodding brown seed heads

Bloom: Jul–Oct

Cycle/Origin: perennial; native

Zone/Habitat: grasslands and montane at 5,000–8,500' (1,525–2,590 m); among grasses, openings in pine forests

Range: northeastern two-thirds and the southern edge of Arizona

Notes: This onion has the widest range of any of the many species in the genus *Allium*. It is native to North America, ranging northwest to British Columbia, northeast to New York, and east to Georgia. It's one of the few onions grown for its flowers, although the edible bulb does taste like a common garden onion. The 2–5 bulbs per plant can be divided to grow new plants, or it can be grown from seed. Drought tolerant once established, it has been used to treat croup, fever, kidney stones, or respiratory disorders.

CLUSTER TYPE **Round**   FLOWER TYPE **Bell**   LEAF TYPE **Simple**   LEAF ATTACHMENT **Basal**   FRUIT **Pod**

Wild Bergamot
Monarda fistulosa

Family: Mint (Lamiaceae)

Height: 2–4' (61–122 cm)

Flower: many pale-lavender flowers in a round cluster, 1–2" (2.5–5 cm) wide; each flower, 1" (2.5 cm) long, has 2 petals (lips) with the upper lip tipped with a tuft of hairs; clusters sit atop the stems and branches

Leaf: lance-shaped leaves, 1–3" (2.5–7.5 cm) long, that taper to pointed tips and have coarse-toothed margins; each leaf is on a short leafstalk, oppositely attached to a square red stem

Bloom: Jun–Sep

Cycle/Origin: perennial; native

Zone/Habitat: riparian deciduous and montane at 5,000–8,000' (1,525–2,440 m); old fields, moist wooded slopes, forest edges, roadsides

Range: eastern two-thirds of Arizona

Notes: Also called horsemint or bee balm, this is a tall single-stemmed plant of open areas and roadsides. Look for its square stems and oppositely attached leaves to help identify. It emits a strong scent when any part of the plant is rubbed or crushed. The fragrance of the blooms attracts many insects. "Bergamot" refers to a small citrus tree that produces a scent similar to that of this plant. It has been used in folk medicine to make a mint tea to treat many respiratory and digestive ailments; its oil is an essential flavoring in Earl Grey tea.

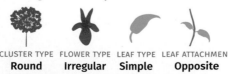

CLUSTER TYPE	FLOWER TYPE	LEAF TYPE	LEAF ATTACHMENT
Round	**Irregular**	**Simple**	**Opposite**

Goodding Verbena
Glandularia gooddingii

Family: Verbena (Verbenaceae)

Height: 12–24" (30–61 cm)

Flower: violet-to-pink flat cluster, 1–3" (2.5–7.5 cm) wide, of many small flowers, ½" (1 cm) wide; each flower looks like a gingerbread man with its 5 notched, slightly different-shaped petals

Leaf: hairy arrowhead-shaped leaves, 1½" (4 cm) long, are dark grayish green, have toothed margins or are divided into lobes, are oppositely attached to the square stems

Bloom: Feb–Oct

Cycle/Origin: perennial; native

Zone/Habitat: desert scrub and riparian, deciduous below 5,000' (1,525 m); slopes, mesas, roadsides, along washes

Range: throughout

Notes: Goodding verbena is a desert plant, but it is dependent upon rainfall and also commonly grows near Arizona's rare desert streams. The showy flowers of this low-mounding plant attract butterflies, making it a favorite landscaping plant in the state. It's also known as southwestern mock vervain or desert verbena. Dakota mock vervain (pg. 169) is similar, but it has leaves with deeply cut, thin lobes and is found at higher elevations than Goodding verbena. Native to the American Southwest in lower elevation deserts, this plant is hardy in temperatures as low as 0°F (-18°C).

CLUSTER TYPE
Flat

FLOWER TYPE
Irregular

LEAF TYPE
Simple

LEAF TYPE
Simple Lobed

LEAF ATTACHMENT
Opposite

Desert Sand Verbena
Abronia villosa

Family: Four O'clock (Nyctaginaceae)

Height: 1–6' (.3–1.8 m)

Flower: round, deep-purple-to-pink clusters, 1–3" (2.5–7.5 cm) wide, made up of 15–35 small tubular flowers of fused petal-like sepals flaring widely into 5 heart-shaped, purple or pink lobes with white bases; on erect, hairy, reddish flower stalks

Leaf: hairy, triangular to oval, grayish-green leaves, ½–4" (1–10 cm) long, are on stalks and feel moist and sticky to the touch

Fruit: rounded triangular brown pod, ½" (1 cm) long, has wrinkled skin and is spongy inside

Bloom: Feb–Jul

Cycle/Origin: annual; native

Zone/Habitat: desert scrub below 3,000' (915 m); along roads, flats, dunes, sandy soils

Range: southwestern quarter of Arizona and the northwestern corner of the state

Notes: This bright wildflower has many reddish multibranching stems that sprawl across the ground. It forms large loose mats of hairy succulent foliage with blooms atop upright flower stalks. It's often found with dune evening-primrose (pg. 267), especially after heavy winter rains, when these species carpet the open desert. *Villosa* means "hairy," referring to the stems, leaves, and blossoms.

CLUSTER TYPE	FLOWER TYPE	LEAF TYPE	LEAF ATTACHMENT	FRUIT
Round	**Tube**	**Simple**	**Opposite**	**Pod**

Dakota Mock Vervain

Glandularia bipinnatifida

Family: Verbena (Verbenaceae)

Height: 6–18" (15–45 cm)

Flower: violet-to-pink flat cluster, 1½" (4 cm) wide, of many small flowers, ½" (1 cm) wide; each flower looks like a gingerbread man with its 5 notched petals that are each a slightly different shape

Leaf: dark-green or bluish-green leaves, 1½" (4 cm) long, are hairy and deeply cut into lobes, with edges curled under, oppositely attached to the hairy stem

Bloom: May–Sep

Cycle/Origin: annual, perennial; native

Zone/Habitat: grasslands, oak/pinyon pine/juniper woodlands, montane and subalpine at 5,000–10,000' (1,525–3,050 m); forest clearings, under trees, along roads

Range: throughout

Notes: The abundant nectar of the showy, long-blooming flowers attracts butterflies, thus this plant is frequently cultivated in butterfly or rock gardens. Dakota mock vervain is hardy and drought tolerant. Its sprawling stems result in mats covering large barren areas, making the plant a good choice for ground cover. In the wild in Arizona, it is often found carpeting the ground under evergreen oaks in the upper elevations of the grasslands or under pines in other life zones.

CLUSTER TYPE
Flat

FLOWER TYPE
Irregular

LEAF TYPE
Simple Lobed

LEAF ATTACHMENT
Opposite

Lambert Locoweed
Oxytropis lambertii

Family: Pea or Bean (Fabaceae)

Height: 5–16" (12.7–40.6 cm)

Flower: pinkish-purple, upright spikes, 1½–4" (4–10 cm); each pea-like flower, ½–1" (1.3–2.5 cm) long, has an erect upper petal (banner) notched at the tip, with rolled back sides, and a pale patch in the center; a lower petal (keel) forms a tiny beak

Leaf: silvery-green basal leaves, 6–12" (15.2–30.5 cm) long, usually with long silky hairs, divided into 7–17 pointed leaflets attached to the long leafstalk in opposite pairs

Fruit: leathery, upright, beaked pod, ½–1¼" (1.3–3.2 cm) long, covered with white hairs

Bloom: Jun–Sep

Cycle/Origin: perennial; native

Zone/Habitat: sandy soils, in open places among ponderosa pine forests at 5,000–8,000' (1,524–2,438 m)

Range: northeastern two-thirds of Arizona, and southeastern and south-central counties

Notes: On this showy flower, the leaves are attached basally, but they can be so long that the lack of a plant stem is not obvious. Locoweeds (*Oxytropis* species) resemble the related milkvetches (*Astragalus* species), but they lack stems and have longer white, silky hairs on the flower stalks and leaves. Also called purple locoweed, it is one of the locoweeds most frequently responsible for livestock poisoning, as it contains a toxin called swansinine.

CLUSTER TYPE
Spike

FLOWER TYPE
Irregular

LEAF TYPE
Compound

LEAF ATTACHMENT
Basal

FRUIT
Pod

171

Arizona Lupine
Lupinus arizonicus

Family: Pea or Bean (Fabaceae)

Height: 4–20" (10–50 cm)

Flower: fuzzy spike cluster, 1¾–9½" (4–24 cm) long, of pealike pinkish-purple flowers, each ½" (1 cm) long; upper petal (standard) has a white spot with yellow center, lower petal (keel) solid pink with long hairs below

Leaf: each bright-green, succulent-like leaf has 6–9 pointed leaflets arranged in a finger-like spread; leaves are 1–1½" (2.5–4 cm) long, on long stalks and alternate on the hairy, branching stems

Fruit: hairy, upright seedpod, ¾" (2 cm) long, grows on one side of spike

Bloom: Jan–May

Cycle/Origin: annual; native

Zone/Habitat: sandy washes, roadsides, 100–3,000' (30–915 m)

Range: south-central and all along the western border of Arizona

Notes: This lupine grows in very low deserts and has flowers that are pinkish purple instead of the usual blue to bluish purple. The upper petal has a white spot with a yellow center dotted in brown that turns deep magenta with fertilization. Unlike the other 23 species of lupines in Arizona, the lower petals, seedpod, and stems are very hairy and the leaves are smooth above and semi-succulent in thickness.

CLUSTER TYPE **Spike**	FLOWER TYPE **Irregular**	LEAF TYPE **Palmate**	LEAF ATTACHMENT **Alternate**	LEAF ATTACHMENT **Basal**	FRUIT **Pod**

173

Texas Toadflax
Nuttallanthus texanus

Family: Snapdragon (Scrophulariaceae)

Height: 6–28" (15–71 cm)

Flower: loose spike clusters, 2½" (6 cm) long, of 10–12 pale-lavender flowers; each blossom, ½" (1 cm) long, on a short stalk, has a 2-lobed upper petal (lip) and a 3-lobed horizontal lower lip with a conspicuous, downward-curving spur

Leaf: few slender, stalkless leaves, ½–1" (1–2.5 cm) long, scattered along the upright, slender, flowering stalk; slightly broader leaves are oppositely attached or whorled (forming a rosette) on the long prostrate stems at base of stalk

Bloom: Mar–Jun

Cycle/Origin: annual, biennial; native

Zone/Habitat: desert scrub, chaparral, semidesert grasslands at 1,500–5,000' (457–1,520 m); in dry sandy soils, along arroyos, roadsides, stream banks, and grassy hills

Range: southern half of Arizona

Notes: Toadflaxes are easily identified by their long spurs, which contain nectar that attracts pollinating insects, and are often referred to as spurred snapdragons. The genus name is for Thomas Nuttall, premier naturalist of the early 1800s. Widespread across much of the United States, it's frequently seen in wildflower gardens, where the pretty, delicate flowers attract bees and butterflies. Caterpillars of buckeye butterflies eat the foliage.

CLUSTER TYPE
Spike

FLOWER TYPE
Irregular

LEAF TYPE
Simple

LEAF ATTACHMENT
Alternate

LEAF ATTACHMENT
Basal

Violet Wild Petunia
Ruellia nudiflora

Family: Acanthus (Acanthaceae)

Height: 12–24" (30–61cm)

Flower: loose clusters of broadly trumpet-shaped, lavender flowers; each flower, 2–2½" (3–6.4 cm) long and 2" (5 cm) wide, has 5 wide wrinkled petals (two above, three below) and each centrally streaked with dark purple

Leaf: bright-green, oval-to-lance-shaped leaves, 2–5" (1–7.5 cm) long, with smooth or wavy, irregularly toothed edges and definite veins; pairs of leaves are oppositely attached to the slender stems

Fruit: slender, upright, pointed pod, ½–1" (1.3–2.5 cm) long, turning brown and woody when mature, then opening explosively to expel seeds

Bloom: May–Oct, especially after monsoon rains

Cycle/Origin: perennial; native

Zone/Habitat: desert scrub and desert grassland, moist shaded canyons, 1,500–4,500' (457–1372 m); along washes, streambeds

Range: southern, central Arizona

Notes: An upright, thin-stemmed plant with broader, greener leaves than most Sonoran Desert natives. Found in moist, shaded areas under mesquite trees and along rare desert streams. Many kinds of butterflies drink the nectar and use the leaves as caterpillar forage. The blooms of violet wild petunia resemble those of the commonly potted petunia, but they are not related.

FLOWER TYPE **Tube**   LEAF TYPE **Simple**   LEAF ATTACHMENT **Opposite**   FRUIT **Pod**

Rocky Mountain Iris
Iris missouriensis

Family: Iris (Iridaceae)

Height: 8–20" (20–50 cm)

Flower: several large, bluish-purple flowers, 2–4" (5–10 cm) wide, atop tall stiff stalks; 3 mostly solid-colored, erect petals; 3 drooping petal-like sepals, heavily veined, darker purple with beardless centers and white patches (throats) trimmed in yellow

Leaf: flattened grass-like blades, 6–20" (15–50 cm) long and ½" (1 cm) wide, light green with whitish bases

Fruit: wrinkled oblong green pod, 1½–2" (4–5 cm) long, with 6 obvious ridges, turns brown when mature

Bloom: May–Sep

Cycle/Origin: perennial; native

Zone/Habitat: montane and subalpine at 6,000–9,500' (1,830–2,895 m); moist meadows, aspen groves, ditches

Range: northern half of Arizona (except the northwestern corner) and the southeastern corner of the state

Notes: Commonly found throughout the western half of the United States and Canada, this is the only iris native to Arizona. The blooms and leaves resemble those of a garden iris; the flower color varies from dark blue to lavender to white. A paste of the ripe seeds has been used by Shoshone and Paiute Peoples to dress burns. The roots are poisonous and were ground up to make an arrow poison. Avoided by livestock, it tends to overtake land that is heavily grazed.

FLOWER TYPE **Irregular**   LEAF TYPE **Simple**   LEAF ATTACHMENT **Basal**   FRUIT **Pod**

179

Hillside Verbena
Verbena neomexicana

Family: Verbena (Verbenaceae)

Height: 12–30" (30–76 cm)

Flower: thin leafless spikes with maroon buds, 3–7" (7.6–18 cm) long, are densely glandular with small lavender flowers opening first from the base of the spike cluster, then upwards; each blossom, ⅜" (1 cm) long, has 2 upper rounded lips and 3 lower lobed petals around a fuzzy white center

Leaf: grayish-green, hairy, thin leaves, ¾–3½" (2–9 cm) long, are deeply cleft with pointed lobes or have sparse teeth along the edges. Opposite leaf pairs are meagerly scattered on green, coarsely hairy stems that have 4 linear ridges and are held erect in a wide fan

Bloom: Mar–Oct

Cycle/Origin: perennial; native

Zone/Habitat: canyons, limestone cliffs, talus slopes at 2,000–6,000' (610–1,830 m) in desert grasslands, chaparral, among junipers or pinyon pines, or along streams, railroads, and disturbed ground

Range: wide diagonal band across Arizona from the northwest to southeast corners

Notes: Also called hillside vervain, the attractively airy appearance of this plant is caused by the leafless flower stalks and few scattered leaves. It's often found growing under pinyon pines, which improve the soil where they live by increasing the nutrients.

CLUSTER TYPE
Spike

FLOWER TYPE
Irregular

LEAF TYPE
Simple

LEAF TYPE
Simple Lobed

LEAF ATTACHMENT
Opposite

181

Owl's Clover
Castilleja exserta

Family: Broomrape (Orobanchaceae)

Height: 4–16" (10–40 cm)

Flower: dense, pinkish-purple spike, 4–8" (10–20 cm) long, of many small flowers; each bloom, 1" (2.5 cm) long, has 2 rose-purple petals (lips); upper is beak-like and broad lower lip has white, yellow, or darker purple spots; two-toned bracts of maroon and pinkish purple

Leaf: fern-like, grayish-green leaves, ½–2" (1–5 cm) long, are deeply divided into 5–9 thin lobes and covered with sticky, fuzzy white hairs

Bloom: Mar–May

Cycle/Origin: annual; native

Zone/Habitat: desert scrub and grasslands at 1,500–4,500' (460–1,370 m); among creosote bushes, open flats, mesas

Range: parts of southern, central, and western Arizona, covering about half of the state

Notes: This wildflower is especially common in Organ Pipe Cactus National Monument in southwestern Arizona. After good winter rains, masses of owl's clover, mixed with other colorful annuals, cover large areas of desert. This plant may be semiparasitic, getting nourishment from the roots of other desert wildflowers. The seeds are stored (often by harvester ants) in the soil, where they stay dormant for years, until the next heavy winter rainfall. It's frequently cultivated in Arizona.

CLUSTER TYPE
Spike

FLOWER TYPE
Irregular

LEAF TYPE
Simple Lobed

LEAF ATTACHMENT
Alternate

MacDougal Verbena
Verbena macdougalii

Family: Verbena (Verbenaceae)

Height: 24–36" (61–91 cm)

Flower: fuzzy, narrow, purple-and-green spike clusters, 16–18" (40–45 cm) long, of tiny densely-packed purple flowers blooming in rings from the top of the spike downward

Leaf: lance-shaped, dark-green leaves, 3–4" (7.5–10 cm) long, are thick, softly hairy, sharply toothed, and have prominent veins; upper leaves are only slightly smaller than lower leaves

Bloom: Jun–Sep

Cycle/Origin: perennial; native

Zone/Habitat: montane at 6,000–8,500' (1,830–2,590 m); along roads, open areas, flats, grassy meadows, among ponderosa pines

Range: northern half and along the central southern border of Arizona

Notes: It's extremely abundant along highways in northern Arizona. Unlike other species of *Verbena*, this stately plant has many tall showy flower spikes, and its flowers are pollinated by flies and bees rather than butterflies. The flower spikes turn maroon and become furry looking after blooming; then they turn light brown and black and become rough when the tiny seedpods are ripe. Plant parts in this genus have been used as a diuretic, sedative, or muscle relaxant.

CLUSTER TYPE
Spike

FLOWER TYPE
Irregular

LEAF TYPE
Simple

LEAF ATTACHMENT
Opposite

LEAF ATTACHMENT
Clasping

Arizona Thistle
Cirsium arizonicum

Family: Aster (Asteraceae)

Height: 1–5' (30–152 cm)

Flower: as many as 100 red-to-orange (sometimes pink-to-lavender) flower heads per plant; each flower head, ⅝–2" (1.5–5 cm) long, is made up of thin tubular disk flowers held tightly by layers of spiny bracts with a central white line, arranged in a tight spiral

Leaf: highly variable leaves; oblong basal leaves, 1½–12" (4–30 cm) long, have spine-tipped teeth or lobes; stem leaves are usually clasping

Bloom: May–Oct

Cycle/Origin: perennial, biennial; native

Zone/Habitat: desert scrub and pinyon pine/juniper woodlands at 3,000–7,000' (915–2,135 m); foothills, canyons, pinewoods, along roads

Range: northern half and southernmost quarter of Arizona

Notes: Arizona thistle is extremely variable in flower color and the shape of the leaves; the elevation at which it occurs is also variable. However, the flower always appears only partly open because the bracts never allow it to spread into the typical wide disk shape of other thistle species. It attracts hummingbirds and bees, which pollinate the flowers. There are 17 species of thistle in Arizona, all produce seeds that are an important food source for birds, especially northern cardinals and lesser goldfinches.

FLOWER TYPE
Composite

LEAF TYPE
Simple

LEAF TYPE
Simple Lobed

LEAF ATTACHMENT
Alternate

LEAF ATTACHMENT
Clasping

187

Scarlet Cinquefoil
Potentilla thurberi

Family: Rose (Rosaceae)

Height: 24–36" (61–91 cm)

Flower: groups of saucer-shaped, scarlet-red flowers are on tall, almost-leafless flower stalks; each flower, 1" (2.5 cm) wide, has 5 broadly heart-shaped petals with darker red bases and lighter red flower parts

Leaf: hand-shaped basal leaves, 2–4" (5–10 cm) wide, are dark green and divided into 5–7 finely toothed leaflets, ½–2" (1–5 cm) long, with silky hairs below and on long hairy stalks; much smaller stem leaves lack leafstalks and grow in whorls about the stem

Bloom: Jul–Oct

Cycle/Origin: perennial; native

Zone/Habitat: montane, subalpine at 6,000–9,000' (1,830–2,745 m); among coniferous trees, canyons, rich soils

Range: eastern half of Arizona

Notes: Plants in the genus *Potentilla* have five-fingered or palmate leaves, thus the common name "cinquefoil," meaning "five leaves." A medium- to high-elevation plant in Arizona, it is found only in fertile soils among coniferous trees on mountains. Semi-trailing, it spreads somewhat like its close relative, wild strawberry (pg. 219), forming clumps and creating a hardy ground cover. The beautiful, velvety red flowers and dark-green leaves make this an attractive addition to gardens with acid soils in cool climates.

FLOWER TYPE
Regular

LEAF TYPE
Palmate

LEAF ATTACHMENT
Whorl

LEAF ATTACHMENT
Basal

Cardinal Catchfly
Silene laciniata

Family: Pink (Caryophyllaceae)

Height: 12–27" (30–69 cm)

Flower: vivid red flowers, 1–1½" (2.5–4 cm) wide, have 5 deeply fringed petals; each bloom emerges from a tubular, hairy, ridged, reddish calyx, ¾" (2 cm) long

Leaf: lance-to-spoon-shaped leaves, ½–6" (1–15 cm) long, are sticky and hairy; a few upper pairs of widely spaced, narrower, and slightly shorter leaves

Fruit: cylindrical-to-egg-shaped tan capsule, ½" (1 cm) long, with reddish-brown seeds

Bloom: Jul–Oct

Cycle/Origin: perennial; native

Zone/Habitat: interior chaparral, oak/pinyon pine/juniper woodlands, montane at 5,500–9,000' (1,675–2,745 m); grassy and brushy slopes

Range: eastern two-thirds of Arizona

Notes: Widely cultivated for its showy, serrated flowers, this long-blooming plant is easily grown from seed. If planted in early spring, it will bloom the same summer. Its nectar contains about 75% sucrose (ideal for attracting hummingbirds), and the plant is often pollinated by Anna's hummingbirds. Many members of *Silene* are collectively referred to as catchflies, as the foliage is sticky enough to trap insects. In the wild, it ranges from southern California to the southwestern corner of Texas (Big Bend area) and into Mexico.

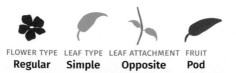

FLOWER TYPE **Regular**   LEAF TYPE **Simple**   LEAF ATTACHMENT **Opposite**   FRUIT **Pod**

Arizona Honeysuckle

Lonicera arizonica

Family: Honeysuckle (Caprifoliaceae)

Height: 3–18' (.9–5.5 m); vine

Flower: groups of 3–12 tubular orangish-red flowers tip the stem; each bloom, 1–1½" (2.5–4 cm) long, has a narrow yellow throat and barely protruding flower parts

Leaf: oval, sticky, finely hairy, bluish-green leaves, 2–3" (5–7.5 cm) long; 1 to several stalkless pairs of upper leaves are joined at their bases

Fruit: clusters of oval, shiny red berries

Bloom: Jun–Jul

Cycle/Origin: perennial; native

Zone/Habitat: riparian deciduous, montane, subalpine at 6,000–9,000' (1,830–2,745 m); open ponderosa pine forests, under firs or maples, canyons, partial shade

Range: most of the eastern two-thirds of Arizona

Notes: This honeysuckle is one of many species of wildflowers in Arizona that have reddish tubular flowers pollinated by any of the 13 species of hummingbirds found in the state. Researchers have discovered that hummingbirds in the White Mountains carry pollen simultaneously from as many as four different wildflower species with similar-looking, tubular red blooms. Differences in the tube shapes and lengths of the flower parts determine where on the bodies of the birds the pollen is deposited. Thus, the pollen right for a flower species is brushed off on the next corresponding species.

FLOWER TYPE	LEAF TYPE	LEAF ATTACHMENT	FRUIT
Tube	**Simple**	**Opposite**	**Berry**

Firecracker Penstemon
Penstemon eatoni

Family: Plantain (Plantaginaceae)

Height: 16–36" (40–91 cm)

Flower: eye-catching spike cluster, 1–1½" (2.5–4 cm) long, of scarlet-red flowers; each flower is tubular with 5 equal lobes (lower lobe is curved downward); pairs of flowers grow along 1 side of flower stalk

Leaf: broadly lance-shaped or oval basal leaves, 1–3½" (2.5–9 cm) long, are dark green and leathery; stem leaves (cauline) are opposite and much smaller on upper stem

Bloom: Feb–Jun

Cycle/Origin: perennial; native

Zone/Habitat: desert scrub, pinyon/juniper woods, montane at 2,000–7,000' (610–2,135 m); among sagebrush or coniferous trees, along roads, riverbanks, slopes

Range: northern half and south-central third of Arizona

Notes: Most penstemons have five male flower parts (stamens) and are commonly called "beardtongues" for their hairy fifth sterile stamen. However, the fifth stamen of firecracker penstemon has few or no hairs. The flowers provide a nectar source in early spring, attracting butterflies and hummingbirds. There are 13 species of colorful hummingbirds found regularly in Arizona, so planting and tending hummingbird gardens around homes is a popular pastime in the state. It's also called scarlet bugler.

CLUSTER TYPE
Spike

FLOWER TYPE
Tube

LEAF TYPE
Simple

LEAF ATTACHMENT
Opposite

LEAF ATTACHMENT
Basal

Firecrackerbush

Bouvardia ternifolia

Family: Madder (Rubiaceae)

Height: 2–4' (61–122 cm); shrub

Flower: slender, tubular, vermilion-red flowers, 1–2" (2.5–5 cm) long, with petals flaring into 4 pointed lobes; in upright groups at the tips of the leafy branches

Leaf: lance-shaped, dark-green leaves, 1–3" (2.5–7.5 cm) long, with pointed tips, grow in closely spaced whorls of 3 about the white-barked stem

Fruit: groups of small round green capsules, turning tan, ¼" (.6 cm) wide, are suspended on short stems and have many tiny brown seeds

Bloom: May–Oct

Cycle/Origin: perennial; native

Zone/Habitat: riparian deciduous at 3,000–9,000' (915–2,745 m); canyons, mountain slopes

Range: southeastern quarter of Arizona

Notes: In the United States, this mostly tropical plant is native only to southeastern Arizona, southern New Mexico, and western Texas, but it ranges far south into Mexico and Central America. It's common along streams in canyons of Arizona, especially in Madera Canyon, a popular birding spot located south of Tucson that is famous for its many species of hummingbirds. As a cultivated shrub, it is well liked because it attracts hummingbirds to its honeysuckle-like flowers, which bloom profusely and continuously through the summer.

FLOWER TYPE	LEAF TYPE	LEAF ATTACHMENT	FRUIT
Tube	**Simple**	**Whorl**	**Pod**

Woolly Indian Paintbrush
Castilleja lanata

Family: Broomrape (Orobanchaceae)

Height: 12–36" (30–91 cm)

Flower: spike cluster, 1–4" (2.5–10 cm) long, of inconspicuous tubular red, yellow, and green flowers, 1" (2.5 cm) long, interspersed among 3-lobed, woolly, leafy bracts; bracts are tipped with bright orangish red and are often mistaken for flower petals

Leaf: narrow pointed leaves, ½–2" (1–5 cm) long, are greenish gray and covered with dense white hairs; leaves alternate at widely spaced intervals

Fruit: small pod-like green container, ½" (1 cm) long

Bloom: Mar–Aug

Cycle/Origin: perennial; native

Zone/Habitat: desert scrub at 2,500–6,500' (760–1,980 m); flats

Range: southernmost quarter of Arizona

Notes: The leaves and stems of this perennial are covered with dense, intertwined, long white hairs, thus "woolly" in the common name. The fresh or dried leaves were once used by the Zapotec People of Mexico when cooking beans or rice. It can be cultivated, but it is semiparasitic and needs to be planted near other species to absorb nutrients from their roots. It's pollinated mainly by hummingbirds, which are attracted by the red bracts, but they get nectar from the tubular flowers. It ranges from California east to Texas and south into Mexico.

CLUSTER TYPE	FLOWER TYPE	LEAF TYPE	LEAF ATTACHMENT	FRUIT
Spike	**Tube**	**Simple**	**Alternate**	**Pod**

Beloperone
Justicia californica

Family: Acanthus (Acanthaceae)

Height: 3–6' (.9–1.8 m); shrub

Flower: pairs of tubular, brick-red flowers; each narrow flower, 2" (5 cm) long, has 5 fused petals with a notched upper lip and 3-lobed lower lip; 2 white-tipped male flower parts (anthers) project from tube

Leaf: hairy, pale-green, oval leaves, ½–3" (1–7.5 cm) long, are evergreen, with pointed tips and wavy margins; oppositely attached to fuzzy stems

Fruit: club-shaped green pod, turning brown, ½" (1 cm) long, opens explosively to expel 2 seeds

Bloom: Mar–Jun

Cycle/Origin: perennial; native

Zone/Habitat: desert scrub and grasslands at 1,000–4,000' (305–1,220 m); slopes, flats, along washes, canyons, streambeds, planted in landscaping

Range: western third of Arizona

Notes: This plant is often cultivated to provide nectar for the 13–15 hummingbird species that live in or migrate through Arizona. It's also called hummingbird bush or chuparosa, which is Spanish for "hummingbird." Beloperone is a good plant for desert landscaping, tolerating heat and drought and recovering if frozen back to the ground. Leaves are present only when the plant is actively growing, dropping off during drought or cold.

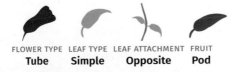

FLOWER TYPE   LEAF TYPE   LEAF ATTACHMENT   FRUIT
Tube   **Simple**   **Opposite**   **Pod**

Cardinal Monkeyflower

Erythranthe cardinalis

Family: Monkeyflower (Phrymaceae)

Height: 10–32" (25–80 cm)

Flower: vivid red-to-orange tubular flower, 2–3" (5–7.5 cm) long, with 2 lips, yellow-streaked throat, and protruding yellow flower parts; upper notched lip arches forward, lower lip has 3 notched lobes bent downward; a few blooms grouped atop stems

Leaf: stalkless, oval, dark-green leaves, 1–3" (2.5–7.5 cm) long, fuzzy, sticky, with coarsely toothed edges and pointed tips; upper leaves clasp fleshy hairy stems

Fruit: oval, ridged, maroon-and-brown pod, ⅔" (1.6 cm) long, contains brown seeds

Bloom: Mar–Oct

Cycle/Origin: perennial; native

Zone/Habitat: riparian deciduous at 1,800–8,500' (550–2,590 m); wet seeps, along or in washes, shade to full sun

Range: throughout, except the southwestern corner

Notes: This moisture-loving wildflower is native throughout the far West from Washington to New Mexico, growing in moist-to-boggy soil. It also grows well in gardens when planted near leaky faucets, birdbaths, or fountains. Easily grown from seed, it spreads widely by underground stems. The showy flowers are magnets for hummingbirds. Caterpillars of checkerspot and Arizona's two species of buckeye butterflies feed on the foliage.

FLOWER TYPE	LEAF TYPE	LEAF ATTACHMENT	LEAF ATTACHMENT	FRUIT
Tube	**Simple**	**Opposite**	**Clasping**	**Pod**

Desert Indian Paintbrush
Castilleja angustifolia

Family: Broomrape (Orobanchaceae)

Height: 6–16" (15–40 cm)

Flower: spike cluster, 2–6" (5–15 cm) long, of inconspicuous tubular green flowers, 1–1½" (2.5–4 cm) long, interspersed among fuzzy leafy bracts with 3–5 lobes; bracts are tipped with bright orangish red and are often mistaken for flower petals

Leaf: nearly clasping, grayish-green-to-purplish leaves, 1–3" (2.5–7.5 cm) long, narrow and hairy, divided into up to 5 pairs of narrow, spreading finger-like lobes

Fruit: small pod-like green container, ½" (1 cm) long

Bloom: Mar–Sep

Cycle/Origin: perennial; native

Zone/Habitat: desert scrub, interior chaparral, oak/pinyon pine/juniper woodlands, montane at 2,000–8,000' (610–2,440 m); among pines or sagebrush scrub

Range: northern two-thirds of Arizona

Notes: It's so named because each stem is topped with bright red, resembling a painter's brush. Thought to be semiparasitic, its roots tap into those of other plants to gain nutrients. It's one of more than a dozen species of *Castilleja* in Arizona. Paintbrushes hybridize often, thus identifying a species can be difficult. It's widespread throughout the West.

CLUSTER TYPE
Spike

FLOWER TYPE
Tube

LEAF TYPE
Simple Lobed

LEAF ATTACHMENT
Alternate

FRUIT
Pod

Hackberry Penstemon
Penstemon subulatus

Family: Snapdragon (Scrophulariaceae)

Height: 1–3' (31–91 cm)

Flower: open spike cluster, 4–16" (10–40 cm) long, of deep-vermilion, tubular flowers; each bloom, ¾–1" (1.8–2.5 cm) long, has 5 fused petals forming a tube, flaring at the mouth with 2 petals above 3 petals, lip of petals sometimes turning yellow with minute red glands; central yellow flower parts do not project beyond the mouth

Leaf: narrow, linear leaves, 3–4" (8–10 cm) long, tapering to a sharp point, oppositely attached in widely spaced pairs on green or purplish-green stems; smooth stems and leaves covered with a grayish-blue, waxy coating that is easily rubbed off

Bloom: Mar–Jun

Cycle/Origin: perennial; native

Zone/Habitat: Sonora Desert middle uplands at 1,970–4,500' (600–1,372 m), on rocky slopes, cliff faces, canyon bottoms, roadsides, and arroyo banks

Range: found only in the western ⅔ of Arizona

Notes: This showy red flower is found in no other state (i.e., it's endemic). It is recognized by pollination ecologists as important to Arizona's many native bees. It can be mistaken for the more widespread firecracker penstemon (pg. 195) but hackberry's fused petals open out more fully at the mouth, bending by 90 degrees or more, and the stamens don't extend past the mouth.

CLUSTER TYPE	FLOWER TYPE	LEAF TYPE	LEAF ATTACHMENT
Spike	**Tube**	**Simple**	**Opposite**

Scarlet Hedge-nettle
Stachys coccinea

Family: Mint (Lamiaceae)

Height: 12–30" (30–76 cm)

Flower: scarlet-red spike cluster, 6–18" (15–45 cm) long, of spaced whorls of 3–6 tubular flowers; each flower, ¾–1½" (2–4 cm) long, has 2 lips; upper lip is erect, while lower lip is broadly 3-lobed and dangling

Leaf: oval, dark-green leaves, 3" (7.5 cm) long, are fuzzy, veined, and toothed with pointed tips; evergreen at lower elevations, turning red in cold temperatures; square stems are covered with soft white hairs

Bloom: Mar–Oct

Cycle/Origin: perennial; native

Zone/Habitat: riparian deciduous at 1,500–8,000' (460–2,440 m); slopes, canyons, moist rich soils

Range: southern half and northeastern edge of Arizona, often planted next to birdbaths and garden fountains in Tucson and Phoenix

Notes: Easily grown in wet spots in gardens, where it blooms for months, this showy wildflower provides gorgeous color and attracts hummingbirds to its nectar. Like other members of the Mint family, it has hairy square stems, two-lipped tubular flowers, and a minty fragrance. It requires moist soil and partial shade to thrive in Arizona, so it is most often found in riparian deciduous canyons in the wild. It's also known as Texas betony or scarlet sage.

CLUSTER TYPE	FLOWER TYPE	LEAF TYPE	LEAF ATTACHMENT
Spike	**Irregular**	**Simple**	**Opposite**

Beardlip Penstemon
Penstemon barbatus

Family: Plantain (Plantaginaceae)

Height: 1–4' (30–122 cm)

Flower: tall spike cluster, 8–18" (20–45 cm) long, of many tubular vermilion-red flowers hanging along 1 side of stem; each narrow flower, 1–1½" (2.5–4 cm) long, has a protruding upper petal (lip), lower lip white streaked at base and bent backward and downward

Leaf: grayish-green basal leaves, 3–5" (7.5–13 cm) long, are sword shaped with pointed tips and slightly wavy margins; stem leaves are opposite

Bloom: Jun–Oct

Cycle/Origin: perennial; native

Zone/Habitat: oak woodlands, montane and subalpine at 4,000–10,000' (1,220–3,050 m); commonly found along roads in northern Arizona, mountain meadows

Range: throughout, except the southwestern corner and scattered locations in southern half of Arizona

Notes: The genus name *Penstemon* is from the Greek words *pente* for "five" and *stemon* for "stamen," referring to the five male flower parts. This species has a yellow-haired tuft covering the whole lower lip, thus the name "beardlip." It has a semi-evergreen basal rosette of leaves, although the flower stalks are deciduous. Oddly-shaped tubular flowers are pollinated almost exclusively by hummingbirds. It's very common in Arizona in the middle and higher elevations.

CLUSTER TYPE
Spike

FLOWER TYPE
Tube

LEAF TYPE
Simple

LEAF ATTACHMENT
Opposite

LEAF ATTACHMENT
Basal

Scarlet Gilia

Ipomopsis aggregata

Family: Phlox (Polemoniaceae)

Height: 16–30" (40–76 cm)

Flower: orangish-red spike clusters, 10–24" (25–61 cm) long, of slim trumpet-shaped flowers, 1½" (4 cm) long; each bloom is red- or yellow-spotted inside, dangles from stem and has 5 long pointed petals that widely flare backward and long protruding flower parts; each blossom held by a small maroon calyx with tapering green-tipped lobes

Leaf: mostly basal, whitish-green leaves, 1–2" (2.5–5 cm) long, are feather-like, woolly, and divided into 9–11 short thin lobes

Bloom: May–Sep

Cycle/Origin: biennial; native

Zone/Habitat: oak/pinyon pine/juniper woods, montane at 5,000–9,000' (1.525–2,756 m); sunny slopes among pines

Range: northern half of and south-central Arizona

Notes: *Aggregata* is Latin for "brought together," referring to the flowers clustering on the unbranched, erect, mostly leafless stems. The showy, odorless blooms are pollinated by hummingbirds. The leaves smell skunk-like when crushed. A basal rosette of leaves persists on the forest floor in winter its first year and withers before blooming in its second summer. Sometimes meadows are colored bright scarlet with large numbers of these blooming plants.

CLUSTER TYPE
Spike

FLOWER TYPE
Tube

LEAF TYPE
Simple Lobed

LEAF ATTACHMENT
Basal

Cardinalflower
Lobelia cardinalis

Family: Bellflower (Campanulaceae)

Height: 2–5' (61–152 cm)

Flower: tall open spike cluster, 12–24" (30–61cm) long, of scarlet-red flowers; each flower, 1½" (4 cm) wide, has 2 upper and 3 spreading lower petals that form a thin tube at its base; flowers alternate on the stem; lower flowers open before upper

Leaf: thin lance-shaped leaves, 2–6" (5–15 cm) long, with toothed margins and pointed tips; purplish-green stem contains a milky sap

Bloom: Jun–Oct

Cycle/Origin: perennial; native

Zone/Habitat: riparian deciduous at 3,000–7,500' (915–2,285 m); along wetlands, meadows, wet soils

Range: throughout, except the southwestern corner

Notes: By far one of the most spectacular wildflowers of Arizona, cardinalflower is found growing in small patches along streams and rivers. It can be grown in backyard oases near water. Its roots need to be wet, and its flowers must have partial shade as well as some sunlight. A short-lived perennial, it differs from penstemons by the alternate leaves (all *Penstemon* spp. have opposite leaves). "Cardinal" refers to Roman Catholic cardinals, whose bright-red robes resemble the scarlet-red color of the flowers. It occasionally produces white or rose-colored blooms. All parts of the plant are poisonous.

CLUSTER TYPE
Spike

FLOWER TYPE
Irregular

LEAF TYPE
Simple

LEAF ATTACHMENT
Alternate

Emory Rock Daisy
Perityle emoryi

Family: Aster (Asteraceae)

Height: 2–24" (5–61 cm)

Flower: familiar round daisy flower head, ½–¾" (1–2 cm) wide, has 8–13 short oval white petals (ray flowers) with notched tips around a wide golden-yellow center (disk flowers)

Leaf: triangular, dark-green leaves, 1–4" (2.5–10 cm) long, are sticky, hairy, succulent, and fragile, with edges irregularly deeply toothed or lobed

Bloom: Feb–Oct

Cycle/Origin: annual; native

Zone/Habitat: desert scrub below 3,000' (915 m); rocky slopes, canyons, arroyos, cracks in cliffs

Range: western two-thirds of Arizona

Notes: This happy-looking daisy with a round face is often seen sprouting from crevices on the sides of cliffs, flowering mostly in the spring but sometimes year-round. Like other short-lived (ephemeral) desert wildflowers, the height and number of Emory rock daisies depend upon the amount of winter rainfall. In years with good winter rains, there are many of these wildflowers, and they grow as tall as 24 inches (61 cm). In drought years, only a few plants germinate from the many seeds stored in the soil and bloom when just a couple of inches tall.

FLOWER TYPE
Composite

LEAF TYPE
Simple

LEAF TYPE
Simple Lobed

LEAF ATTACHMENT
Alternate

217

fruit

Wild Strawberry
Fragaria virginiana

Family: Rose (Roseaceae)

Height: 3–6" (7.5–15 cm)

Flower: groups of 2–10 white flowers; each flower, ½–1" (1–2.5 cm) wide, has 5 separated oval petals around a fuzzy yellow center

Leaf: whitish-green basal leaves, 3–4" (7.5–10 cm) wide, made up of 3 leaflets; each leaflet, ¾" (2 cm) long, is coarsely toothed; leaves sit on a tall hairy stalk

Fruit: green berry, turning bright red, ¼–½" (.6–1 cm) wide

Bloom: May–Oct

Cycle/Origin: perennial; native

Habitat: montane, subalpine at 7,000–11,000' (2,135–3,355 m); meadows, coniferous forest edges, roadsides

Range: northern half and southeastern corner of Arizona

Notes: It's one of the two original species from which cultivated strawberries are derived and one of two wild strawberry species in Arizona. Flowers are larger than those of the garden variety of strawberry, which sometimes escapes into the wild. It often grows in large patches. It spreads primarily by underground runners but also reproduces by seed. Its flowers and fruit are always on stalks separate from the leaves. It produces some of the sweetest of the wild berries. High in vitamin C, the berries can be eaten fresh or made into jam.

FLOWER TYPE
Regular

LEAF TYPE
Compound

LEAF ATTACHMENT
Basal

FRUIT
Berry

Desert Tobacco
Nicotiana obtusifolia

Family: Nightshade (Solanaceae)

Height: 8–32" (20–80 cm)

Flower: tubular, greenish-white-to-cream flower, ½–1" (1–2.5 cm) long, with 5 blunted spreading lobes; held by hairy greenish calyx with 5 pointed lobes

Leaf: hairy, oval-to-lance-shaped leaves, ¾–4" (2–10 cm) long; lower leaves are wider at tips and with short stalks; upper leaves narrower, pointed at tips and clasping; hairy stems and leaves are both sticky

Fruit: oval green pod, turning brown, ⅓–½" (0.8–1 cm) long, contains tiny brown seeds

Bloom: middle Mar–Nov

Cycle/Origin: annual, perennial, biennial; native

Zone/Habitat: desert scrub below 5,900' (1,800 m); along washes, rocky slopes, among creosote bushes

Range: throughout

Notes: The genus *Nicotiana* is named after Jean Nicot, the French ambassador to Portugal, who introduced tobacco to Europe in 1560. Desert tobacco leaves were dried and smoked by early settlers and by Native Americans, who have used the plant for many medicinal purposes and ceremonial rituals. The foliage contains the poisonous alkaloids nicotine, which has been used in insecticides, and anabasine, both of which are toxic to livestock.

FLOWER TYPE **Tube** LEAF TYPE **Simple** LEAF ATTACHMENT **Alternate** FRUIT **Pod**

Texas False Garlic
Nothoscordum bivalve

Family: Amaryllis (Amaryllidaceae)

Height: 8–12" (20–30 cm)

Flower: star-shaped, yellowish-white flowers, ¾" (2 cm) wide, have 6 similar-looking oval pointed sepals and petals with a pink midline stripe below, surrounding a yellow center; 5–12 flowery-smelling blossoms on stalks branching from the top of stem

Leaf: 1–2 thread-like basal leaves, 3–6" (7.5–15 cm) long, are smooth-edged and wither before plant flowers

Bloom: Apr–May

Cycle/Origin: perennial; native

Zone/Habitat: desert scrub, grasslands, oak/pinyon pine/juniper woodlands at 4,000–6,000' (1,220–1,830 m); flats, slopes, shallow hard and gravelly soils

Range: southeastern to central Arizona, ranging over half of the state

Notes: *Nothoscordum* means "false garlic," referring to the bulb from which it grows. It resembles an onion, but it lacks any onion or garlic odor or flavor. It has three parts to its seed capsule, unlike the two-parted capsule of onion and garlic species in the genus *Allium*. Although common, it often goes unnoticed. An abundant spring wildflower after good winter rains, masses of its blooms can carpet desert flats. It can be seen east of the copper mining town of San Manuel, northwest of Tucson.

FLOWER TYPE   LEAF TYPE   LEAF ATTACHMENT
Regular   **Simple**   **Basal**

Canada Violet
Viola canadensis

Family: Violet (Violaceae)

Height: 8–16" (20–40 cm)

Flower: typical violet-shaped white flower, ¾–1" (2–2.5 cm) wide, often tinged pink with age, sits on a slender purplish flower stalk; flowers stand above the leaves

Leaf: heart-shaped leaves, 1–3" (2.5–7.5 cm) wide, with pointed tips and bluntly toothed margins, on thin purplish stalks with sparse hairs

Bloom: Apr–Sep

Cycle/Origin: perennial; native

Zone/Habitat: montane and subalpine at 6,000–11,500' (1,830–3,510 m); coniferous forests, rich moist soils

Range: eastern three-quarters of Arizona, except the south-central part of the state

Notes: One of the few "stalked" violets, the Canada violet flower rises from a stalk that originates from a leaf attachment (axis), rather than the more typical basal flower stalk arrangement of most violets. It grows in patches from aboveground runners, called stolons, and is one of the few violets that has a fragrance. Though it's found only on mountains in Arizona, it is widespread in the United States and ranges north into Canada. Canada violet requires moist soils found in wet ditches along roads; near springs; or in shady places under pine, spruce, or fir trees.

FLOWER TYPE **Irregular** LEAF TYPE **Simple** LEAF ATTACHMENT **Alternate**

lobed ray
flowers

Whitedaisy Tidytips
Layia glandulosa

Family: Aster (Asteraceae)

Height: 4–24" (10–61 cm)

Flower: daisy-like, bright-white flower, ¾–1½" (2–4 cm) wide, made up of 5–7 ray flowers, each tipped with 3 equal lobes surrounding the orange center

Leaf: fuzzy, dark-green leaves, ¼–3" (.6–7.6 cm) long; basal leaves usually spoon-shaped and lobed, stem leaves are thinly linear and alternately attached to hairy, green or purple-streaked, branching stems

Bloom: Feb–Apr

Cycle/Origin: annual; native

Zone/Habitat: dry sand or gravel slopes in upper and lower deserts and grasslands, on mesas, sunny clearings at 0–5,000' (0–1,524 m)

Range: throughout Arizona, except the extreme south-western corner

Notes: Eye-catching even at a distance, one white flower tops each upright stem and waves in the breeze. Like many plants in Arizona, it blooms only when winter rains have been sufficient. So, in drought, it may be totally absent from the landscape. Very important to native bees in Arizona, it is valued in pollinator gardens, and its seeds are commercially available. It's found in western deserts extending north to Washington, west to California, and south to Baja California in Mexico.

FLOWER TYPE
Composite

LEAF TYPE
Simple

LEAF TYPE
Simple Lobed

LEAF ATTACHMENT
Alternate

Stemless Townsend Daisy

Townsendia exscapa

Family: Aster (Asteraceae)

Height: 1–3" (2.5–7.5 cm)

Flower: white flower head, ¾–2" (2–5 cm) wide, has 20–40 long narrow white petals (ray flowers) and a yellow center (disk flowers); petals are pale pink below

Leaf: long and narrow or spoon-shaped, grayish-haired, dark-green leaves, 1–3" (2.5–7.5 cm) long, in a dense basal rosette; evergreen, wintering as a small ball of leaves protecting the flower buds, which form in fall

Bloom: Mar–Aug

Cycle/Origin: perennial; native

Zone/Habitat: grasslands, oak/pinyon pine/juniper woodlands and montane at 4,500–7,500' (1,370–2,285 m); openings among ponderosa pines or oaks, rock crevices

Range: throughout, except the southwestern quarter

Notes: These very short perennials, which grow in leafy compact mounds a few inches wide, are aptly named *exscapa*, Latin for "without a stem." The large flower heads seem too big for the plant. It's a member of the Aster family, one of the largest plant families in the world. "Aster" means "star" in Greek, referring to the arrangement of the petals, radiating out from the center. Widespread throughout the western half of the United States, it can be found northwest of Walnut Canyon National Monument along the Arizona Trail, a hiking trail running the entire length of the state.

FLOWER TYPE **Composite**   LEAF TYPE **Simple**   LEAF ATTACHMENT **Basal**

Fendler Sandwort

Eremogone fendleri

Family: Pink (Caryophyllaceae)

Height: 3–7" (7.5–18 cm)

Flower: small groups of white flowers top long thin fuzzy stalks; each flower, 1" (2.5 cm) wide, has 5 separated oval petals; 5 pointed, grayish-green bracts

Leaf: long, thread-like, dark-green, mostly basal leaves, ½–2½" (1–6 cm) long, are sharply pointed and sticky; some leaves oppositely attached to stems

Bloom: Apr–Sep

Cycle/Origin: perennial; native

Zone/Habitat: montane and subalpine at 6,000–11,500' (1,830–3,510 m); at the bases of rock piles, coniferous forests, meadows

Range: northern half of Arizona and the mountains in the far southeastern part of the state

Notes: This perennial grows in compact, dark-green mounds. Found in five states, from Arizona north to Wyoming and east to Texas, it is most common in Arizona, Colorado, and Utah. In northeastern Arizona, it is easy to find on slopes throughout the popular Canyon de Chelly National Monument, a unique park comprised entirely of tribal lands belonging to the Navajo Nation. People have occupied this scenic canyon continuously for 1,200 years. The Navajo have used Fendler sandwort to treat respiratory ailments.

FLOWER TYPE **Regular**　LEAF TYPE **Simple**　LEAF ATTACHMENT **Basal**

231

flat stamens

Cream Cup
Platystemon californicus

Family: Poppy (Papaveraceae)

Height: 4–12" (10–30 cm)

Flower: creamy-white-to-pale-yellow flower, 1" (2.5 cm) wide, has 6 oval, flat petals surrounding a mounded cream center; flower atop a long leafless, hairy stem

Leaf: grass-like, grayish-green leaves, ½–3½" (1–9 cm) long, are hairy; the shaggy leaves are mostly on the lower part of the plant

Fruit: cylindrical green capsule, ⅔" (1.6 cm) long, turns brown and contains black seeds

Bloom: Mar–May

Cycle/Origin: annual; native

Zone/Habitat: desert scrub, grasslands, interior chaparral, oak woodlands at 1,500–4,500' (460–1,370 m); along washes, slopes, open grassy areas, moist soils

Range: two-thirds of Arizona, in a wide band from the northwestern to southeastern parts of the state

Notes: The stalks of the male flower parts (stamens) are flattened, thus the genus name *Platystemon*, which combines the Greek words *platus* for "broad" and *stemon* for "stamen." After good winter rains, this small multi-stemmed poppy often blooms among other desert annuals, such as the arroyo lupine (pg. 43) and California poppy (pg. 363), but it is often overlooked because its pale, creamy-white color is overwhelmed by the bright colors of the other flowers.

FLOWER TYPE
Regular

LEAF TYPE
Simple

LEAF ATTACHMENT
Opposite

FRUIT
Pod

233

Richardson Geranium
Geranium richardsonii

Family: Geranium (Geraniaceae)

Height: 8–18" (20–45 cm)

Flower: white-to-pinkish flowers, 1" (2.5 cm) wide, have 5 rounded teardrop-shaped (sometimes drooping) petals streaked with lavender or pink veins, whitish-haired bases, a green center, and upright flower parts

Leaf: maple-like, dark-green leaves, 2–6" (5–15 cm) wide, are stalked, divided into 3–5 main diamond-shaped lobes; upper leaves are smaller

Fruit: long and narrow, erect pointed container, ¾" (2 cm) long, shaped like a crane's bill, contains 1 seed that is lipped with an elongated coiled tail

Bloom: Apr–Oct

Cycle/Origin: perennial; native

Zone/Habitat: riparian deciduous, montane, subalpine at 6,500–11,500' (1,980–3,510 m); meadows, moist soils

Range: northern half of Arizona, except the northwestern and southeastern corners of the state

Notes: It's one of the most common and longest-flowering plants along Arizona's mountain streams and hiking trails, such as the beautiful Oak Creek Canyon Trail near Sedona, Arizona. This low-growing perennial is found in coniferous forests wherever moist soils are present, sometimes nearly covering the forest floor. The dark-green leaves turn red in the fall, making a striking carpet.

FLOWER TYPE
Regular

LEAF TYPE
Simple Lobed

LEAF ATTACHMENT
Opposite

FRUIT
Pod

Rocky Mountain Pussytoes
Antennaria parvifolia

Family: Aster (Asteraceae)

Height: 3–6" (7.5–15 cm)

Flower: loose round cluster, 1" (2.5 cm) wide, made up of 2–7 fuzzy white (sometimes pinkish) flower heads, ½" (1 cm) long; flower heads sit on top of a single fuzzy stem

Leaf: basal leaves, ½–1½" (1–4 cm) long, narrowly spoon-shaped, and covered with white hairs, giving a fuzzy look, a few smaller pointed leaves on the stem

Bloom: May–Aug

Cycle/Origin: perennial; native

Zone/Habitat: montane and subalpine at 6,000–11,500' (1,830–3,510 m); openings among pines, sandy soils

Range: northeastern two-thirds and southeastern corner of Arizona

Notes: The bristly flower heads of this mountain aster resemble a cat's paw, hence the common name. A dense covering of hairs gives a grayish-green color to the leaves and stems. It often grows to form a dense mat, pushing up through a layer of pine needles. It is an allelopathic plant, giving off chemicals that "poison" the soil for other plants, reducing competition for the limited moisture and sunlight on the forest floor. Rocky Mountain pussytoes has fewer and larger blooms and is shorter than the other five species of pussytoes in Arizona.

CLUSTER TYPE
Round

FLOWER TYPE
Composite

LEAF TYPE
Simple

LEAF ATTACHMENT
Alternate

LEAF ATTACHMENT
Basal

Desert Pincushion
Chaenactis stevioides

Family: Aster (Asteraceae)

Height: 2–12" (5–30 cm)

Flower: white-to-pinkish-white flower head, 1" (2.5 cm) wide, of many tiny disk flowers that are larger at the outside rim; sticky, fuzzy, cone-shaped green bract

Leaf: elliptical basal leaves, ½–4½" (1–11 cm) long, larger leaves are divided once or twice into 4–8 pairs of short thin lobes; stem leaves gradually smaller going up stem; basal leaves wither before the plant flowers

Bloom: Mar–Jun

Cycle/Origin: annual; native

Zone/Habitat: desert scrub at 1,000–4,000' (305–1,220 m); shrub-lands among creosote bushes, flats, slopes

Range: throughout

Notes: Desert pincushion is the most abundant spring flower in the upper Mojave Desert, and it's also very common in the Sonoran Desert. The central part of the flower head is composed of partially opened, yellowish or cream-colored disk flowers that turn white when fully open. Disk flowers around the outside edge of the flower cluster are often larger than the central disk flowers. A lookalike species, Fremont pincushion (*C. fremontii*) (not shown), is more abundant in the lower Mojave and northern Sonoran, has fewer stems, fewer flower heads per stem, and paler green bracts than desert pincushion.

FLOWER TYPE
Composite

LEAF TYPE
Simple Lobed

LEAF ATTACHMENT
Alternate

LEAF ATTACHMENT
Basal

239

Desert Anemone
Anemone tuberosa

Family: Buttercup (Ranunculaceae)

Height: 5–16" (13–33 cm)

Flower: white-to-pale-lavender (or pinkish) flowers, 1½" (4 cm) wide; each bloom lacks petals but has 5–11 elliptical petal-like sepals around a fuzzy, green-and-pinkish-lavender center; the sepals are finely hairy below; 1–5 flowers atop a single erect long stalk

Leaf: few basal frilly leaves, 2–4" (5–10 cm) long, on stalks and divided 1–2 times into stalkless lobed leaflets; 3 stem leaves in a whorl at midstem

Bloom: Feb–Mar

Cycle/Origin: perennial; native

Zone/Habitat: desert scrub at 2,500–5,000' (760–1,525 m); rocky slopes, cliff ledges, partial shade

Range: two-thirds of Arizona, in a wide band from the northwestern to southeastern parts of the state

Notes: Although it often goes unnoticed, this early spring wildflower has fairly large blossoms. The brown, woolly, cylindrical seed head, ½–1 inches (1–2.5 cm) long, produces seed-like fruits that are dispersed by the wind, thus it is sometimes called windflower. The plant ranges in the southwestern United States from California to Texas and north to Utah and Nevada. It also occurs in Mexico. A good place to see desert anemone is along the Proctor Road Nature Trail in Madera Canyon, south of Tucson.

FLOWER TYPE
Regular

LEAF TYPE
Compound

LEAF TYPE
Twice Compound

LEAF ATTACHMENT
Whorl

LEAF ATTACHMENT
Basal

241

fruit

Devil's Claw
Proboscidea parviflora

Family: Martynia (Martyniaceae)

Height: 1–3' (30–91 cm)

Flower: white-and-purple tubular flower, 1½" (4 cm) long, has a yellow line in throat and 2 lips divided into 5 lobes; 2 upper lobes, pointed and erect with purplish blotches; lower 3 lobes are slightly streaked inside with pink

Leaf: fuzzy, broadly triangular, long-stalked leaves, 2–6" (5–15 cm) wide, wrinkled with scalloped, toothed, or lobed edges; hairy, sticky reddish branches

Fruit: fuzzy curved okra-like pod, 7" (18 cm) long, dries and splits lengthwise into 2 curving sharp "claws"

Bloom: Apr–Oct

Cycle/Origin: annual; native

Zone/Habitat: desert scrub and grasslands at 1,000–5,000' (305–1,525 m); frequent near ancient Indigenous villages

Range: throughout Arizona, except the southwestern and northeastern corners of the state

Notes: It's named for its split, curved dry pods that resemble sharp claws and catch on the legs of passing animals or on the heels of hikers, dispersing the seeds. Native Americans of the Southwest grow this plant for the dry pod's fibers, which are used in basketry. The pepper-shaped green seedpods and the ripe seeds are said to be edible. A yellow line in the flower's throat guides bees to the nectar.

FLOWER TYPE **Tube** LEAF TYPE **Simple** LEAF ATTACHMENT **Alternate** FRUIT **Pod**

seed heads

Apache Plume
Fallugia paradoxa

Family: Rose (Rosaceae)

Height: 3–5' (.9–1.5 m); shrub

Flower: upright, rose-like white flower, 1–1½" (2.5–4 cm) wide, has 5 broad, slightly unequal-sized petals and a wide greenish-yellow center of many long flower parts; borne singly or in small groups on long stalks

Leaf: clusters of small stiff leaves, ½" (1 cm) long, are dark green above and rusty below, divided into 3–7 rounded lobes; semi-evergreen, turning bronze and dropping during drought

Bloom: Apr–Oct

Cycle/Origin: perennial; native

Zone/Habitat: grasslands, oak/pinyon pine/juniper woodlands and montane at 3,000–8,000' (915–2,440 m); dry rocky slopes, arroyos, near seeps

Range: throughout Arizona, except the northeastern and southwestern corners of the state

Notes: This common, straggly, multi-stemmed shrub is more noted for its tailed seeds than its flowers. The numerous seed heads are tipped by long, densely hairy, tail-like plumes that are 1–2 inches (2.5–5 cm) long (see inset). The feathery pink plumes make the plant appear topped with pompons. Named for the plumes, which resemble Apache feather headdresses, its woody stems have been used for arrow shafts and brooms by Indigenous Peoples.

FLOWER TYPE
Regular

LEAF TYPE
Simple Lobed

LEAF ATTACHMENT
Alternate

Desert Zinnia
Zinnia acerosa

Family: Aster (Asteraceae)

Height: 4–10" (10–25 cm); shrub

Flower: daisy-like flower head, 1–1½" (2.5–4 cm) wide, has 4–7 broadly oval, drooping, white or cream petals (ray flowers) with 3-lobed tips around a small protruding yellow center of 8–13 disk flowers

Leaf: rigid, smooth-edged, very narrowly lance-shaped or needle-like leaves, ⅓–¾" (0.8–2 cm) long; leaves and stems are covered with sticky white glands; multibranched stems are sparsely hairy and densely leafy

Bloom: Mar–Nov, but blooms best following winter and summer rains

Cycle/Origin: perennial; native

Zone/Habitat: desert scrub at 800–5,000' (245–1,525 m); flats among creosote bushes, mesas, calcium soils

Range: southern half of Arizona

Notes: This rounded or flat-topped, raggedly dense shrub has many small white flowers covering the surface of the mound. Aptly named desert zinnia for where it is found—in the deserts of the southern United States and northern Mexico. This pleasant, drought-tolerant perennial likes well-drained soils. The species name *acerosa* means "awl-shaped" and refers to the shape of the leaves. The foliage is smelly when crushed. Harvester ants collect the seeds and store them to eat later, coating them with antibiotic saliva to keep them from decaying.

FLOWER TYPE LEAF TYPE LEAF ATTACHMENT
Composite Simple Opposite

247

Blackfoot Daisy
Melampodium leucanthum

Family: Aster (Asteraceae)

Height: 5–16" (13–40 cm)

Flower: daisy-like white flower head, 1–1½" (2.5–4 cm) wide, made up of 8–13 oval petals (ray flowers) with notched blunt tips around a yellow center; single flower head per stalk; many flower heads per plant

Leaf: grayish-green leaves, ¾–1½" (2–4 cm) long, lance-shaped or narrowly oblong, have smooth margins or are sometimes divided into 2–6 shallow lobes; leaves oppositely attached to multibranched stem

Bloom: Mar–Nov

Cycle/Origin: perennial; native

Zone/Habitat: desert scrub, grasslands, oak woodlands at 800–5,000' (360–1,525 m); along roads, slopes, flats, limestone soils

Range: throughout, except the southwestern corner

Notes: Cultivated in gardens and for erosion control in arid regions because of its hardiness and drought tolerance, this mounded evergreen perennial has many daisy-like, honey-scented flower heads per plant. Its long taproot allows it to reach water deep underground. "Black" in the common name is for the color the flower parts turn with age, and "foot" describes the developing seed, which looks like a black foot at the base of the yellow center. The seeds are food for birds in fall and winter.

FLOWER TYPE
Composite

LEAF TYPE
Simple

LEAF TYPE
Simple Lobed

LEAF ATTACHMENT
Opposite

249

Spreading Fleabane
Erigeron divergens

Family: Aster (Asteraceae)

Height: 5–18" (13–45 cm)

Flower: daisy-like, white-to-pinkish or lavender flower head, 1–1½" (2.5–4 cm) wide, of layers of 75–150 overlapping narrow petals surrounding a yellow center; up to 100 flower heads per plant

Leaf: narrowly spoon-shaped, bluish-green basal leaves, ½–3" (1–7.5 cm) long; stem leaves are erect and fuzzy, getting progressively smaller up the stem

Bloom: Apr–Oct

Cycle/Origin: biennial; native

Zone/Habitat: desert scrub, grasslands, oak/pinyon pine woodlands, montane at 1,000–9,000' (305–2,745 m); disturbed areas, flats, among ponderosa pines

Range: throughout

Notes: A short plant with delicate-looking blooms, spreading fleabane is abundant in Arizona deserts. It's one of over 40 species of fleabane in the *Erigeron* genus in the state. Fleabanes are difficult to differentiate from one another due to variations in color, size, and season of bloom. However, they are easily distinguished from other asters by the many narrow, overlapping ray flowers. While spreading fleabane is found in a wide range of elevations, the lavender-flowered Aspen fleabane (*E. speciosus*) (not shown) can be seen mainly in mountain forests.

FLOWER TYPE **Composite** LEAF TYPE **Simple** LEAF TYPE **Simple Lobed** LEAF ATTACHMENT **Alternate** LEAF ATTACHMENT **Basal**

Desert Chicory

Rafinesquia neomexicana

Family: Aster (Asteraceae)

Height: 4–24" (10–61 cm)

Flower: white flower head, 1–1½" (2.5–4 cm) wide, is tinged maroon below and yellow at the bases of the rectangular petals (ray flowers); has overlapping layers of blunt-tipped petals of varying lengths tipped with 5 small lobes; layers of pointed grayish-green bracts

Leaf: grayish-green leaves, 2–6" (5–15 cm) long, have pairs of thin lobes and are alternate; upper leaves are much smaller; hollow stems contain a milky sap

Bloom: middle Feb–Jul

Cycle/Origin: annual; native

Zone/Habitat: desert scrub at 200–3,000' (60–915 m); flats, mesas, among creosote bushes

Range: throughout Arizona, except the north-central and southeastern parts of the state

Notes: This annual has frail flexible stems, so it grows under shrubs, using them for support and shade. Nonetheless, this is one of the more conspicuous flowers of the western deserts. Like the common carnation it resembles, the flower head has ray flowers only, lacking disk flowers; the centers are just yellow pigment at the base of the petals. The flower heads closely resemble the blossoms of white tackstem (*Calycoseris wrightii*) (not shown), but that species has sticky glands on its stems and bracts.

FLOWER TYPE
Composite

LEAF TYPE
Simple Lobed

LEAF ATTACHMENT
Alternate

Bastard Toadflax
Comandra umbellata

Family: Sandalwood (Santalaceae)

Height: 6–16" (15–40 cm)

Flower: compact flat cluster, 1–2" (2.5–5 cm) wide, of 3–6 flowers; each star-shaped flower, ⅜" (.9 cm) wide, is greenish white to pinkish white, made of 4–6 petal-like sepals around a greenish-yellow center

Leaf: many stalkless fleshy leaves, ¾–1½" (2–4 cm) wide, are narrowly oval, grayish green above and pale green below; multibranched stem

Bloom: Apr–Aug

Cycle/Origin: perennial; native

Zone/Habitat: oak woodlands, montane at 4,000–9,000' (1,220–2,745 m); open fields, forest clearings, along roads, rock crevices, meadows

Range: throughout, except the southwestern corner

Notes: A semiparasitic plant, obtaining some of its nutrients from the roots of other plants, its green leaves also use the sun to make some of its own food (photosynthesis). It forms colonies along horizontal underground roots. The greenish-white flowers lack petals, instead displaying petal-like sepals. "Toad" in common plant names has been used to describe any plant that grows in the shade, but it also may come from the word "tod," which is a clump or tuft. Either explanation certainly describes this plant's flowering habit.

CLUSTER TYPE	FLOWER TYPE	LEAF TYPE	LEAF ATTACHMENT
Flat	**Regular**	**Simple**	**Alternate**

Poison Milkweed

Asclepias subverticillata

Family: Dogbane (Apocynaceae)

Height: 1½–4' (45–122 cm)

Flower: flat cluster, 1–2" (2.5–5 cm) wide, of many small, odd-shaped, white-to-greenish-white flowers, ½" (1 cm) wide; flower has 5 lower petals in a flat ring and 5 smaller upper petals raised above, looking like spokes of a wagon wheel; white central column

Leaf: thread-like, dark-green leaves, 5" (13 cm) long, with rolled edges; in whorls of 3–5 leaves at stem joints

Fruit: erect slender flattened pod, 4" (10 cm) long

Bloom: May–Sep

Cycle/Origin: perennial; native

Zone/Habitat: grasslands and montane at 3,000–8,000' (915–2,440 m); among grasses, roadsides, along trails

Range: northern half and southeastern corner of Arizona

Notes: A very abundant plant in northern Arizona, this milkweed contains a white sap that's poisonous to cows, sheep, and horses; even its dried leaves accidentally bound in hay bales are lethal. Queen and monarch butterfly caterpillars eat the toxic leaves with no ill effects, but they, in turn, become poisonous to birds if eaten. Conspicuous yellow, black, and white stripes on these caterpillars warn potential predators to stay away. It's also called horsetail milkweed for its segmented stems, which are like those of horsetails (grass-like sedges).

CLUSTER TYPE
Flat

FLOWER TYPE
Irregular

LEAF TYPE
Simple

LEAF ATTACHMENT
Whorl

FRUIT
Pod

257

Arizona Popcornflower

Plagiobothrys arizonicus

Family: Forget-me-not (Boraginaceae)

Height: 4–16" (10–40 cm)

Flower: coiled, hairy, white spike clusters, 1–2" (2.5–5 cm) long, made up of tiny tubular flowers with 5 rounded petals around a yellowish-white center

Leaf: bristly haired, thick basal leaves, ½–2" (1–5 cm) long, oblong with pointed tips, edged with dark red along middle vein and edges below; a few smaller alternate stem leaves

Bloom: Mar–May

Cycle/Origin: annual, native

Zone/Habitat: desert scrub, grasslands, oak/pinyon pine/juniper woodlands below 5,000' (1,525 m); under oaks, among creosote bushes

Range: throughout Arizona, except the northeastern and southwestern corners of the state

Notes: The leaves contain a purple juice (used as a dye) that shows through at the middle vein and edges as a dark reddish color. The roots and stems also contain the juice, thus it is also called bloodroot or lipstickweed. It's the most widespread in Arizona, but it's also found throughout the Southwest and north to southwestern Utah. It can be seen in the nation's first protected archaeological site, Casa Grande Ruins National Monument, south of Phoenix, which preserves an ancient Hohokam farming community and "Great House."

CLUSTER TYPE
Spike

FLOWER TYPE
Tube

LEAF TYPE
Simple

LEAF ATTACHMENT
Alternate

LEAF ATTACHMENT
Basal

Scruffy Prairie Clover

Dalea albiflora

Family: Pea or Bean (Fabaceae)

Height: 12–24" (30–61 cm)

Flower: tiny pea-like white flowers in a cone-shaped dense spike cluster, 1–2½" (2.5–6 cm) long; each flower made up of 5 petals surrounding 10 long yellow male flower parts (stamens)

Leaf: narrow compound leaves, ½–1½" (1–4 cm) long, made up of 5–9 pairs of leaflets; leaves and stems are covered with tiny fuzzy white hairs

Bloom: Apr–Oct

Cycle/Origin: perennial, native

Zone/Habitat: grasslands, pinyon pine/juniper woodlands and montane at 3,500–7,500' (1,065–2,285 m); forest clearings, along roads and washes

Range: throughout, except the southwestern corner

Notes: Also called white-flowered prairie clover, the tiny flowers bloom from the bottom up on the spike. There are 36 species of prairie clover in the genus *Dalea* in Arizona. These members of the Pea or Bean family have the ability to fix nitrogen into the soil, thus enhancing soil fertility. Like many prairie plants, prairie clovers have roots that penetrate the soil deeply in search of water. The flowers attract many species of bees.

CLUSTER TYPE
Spike

FLOWER TYPE
Irregular

LEAF TYPE
Compound

LEAF ATTACHMENT
Alternate

Alpine Penny Cress
Noccaea fendleri

Family: Mustard (Brassicaceae)

Height: 4–12" (10–30 cm)

Flower: cylindrical dense flower cluster, 1–3" (2.5–7.5 cm) long, usually white, rarely purplish-pink flowers; each bloom, ⅜" (.9 cm) wide, has 4 spoon-shaped petals around green flower parts

Leaf: spoon-shaped basal leaves, ½–1" (1–2.5 cm) long, are toothed; oval succulent stem leaves clasp the unbranching stems at wide intervals

Fruit: stalked, heart-shaped, flattened, reddish-green seedpod, ¼–½" (.6–1 cm) long, has a thread-like tip

Bloom: Feb–Aug

Cycle/Origin: perennial; native

Zone/Habitat: riparian deciduous, montane, subalpine at 4,000–11,500' (1,220–3,510 m); coniferous forests

Range: throughout, except the southwestern corner

Notes: This perennial begins flowering when it's only 1 inch (2.5 cm) tall, but the many unbranched flower stalks do grow taller and continue to bloom. It starts to bloom in early spring in low canyons and keeps flowering through the summer in the higher mountains. It sometimes grows in large patches with few other kinds of wildflowers near it, providing a uniform-colored carpet of white or pink flowers. It's often called wild candytuft.

CLUSTER TYPE
Spike

FLOWER TYPE
Regular

LEAF TYPE
Simple

LEAF ATTACHMENT
Alternate

LEAF ATTACHMENT
Basal

FRUIT
Pod

263

Woolly Plantain
Plantago patagonica

Family: Plantain (Plantaginaceae)

Height: 2–10" (5–25 cm)

Flower: hairy greenish-white spike cluster, 1–5" (2.5–13 cm) long, of tiny crowded flowers interspersed with white-haired pointed green bracts; each blossom has 4 translucent white-to-tan petals around a red center; 1–20 flower spikes per plant

Leaf: hairy, long, narrow basal leaves, 1–6" (2.5–15 cm) long, with pointed tips

Bloom: Feb–Jul

Cycle/Origin: annual; native

Zone/Habitat: grasslands, interior chaparral and oak/pinyon pine/juniper woodlands at 1,000–7,500' (305–2,285 m); along roads, mesas, slopes

Range: throughout, except the southwestern corner

Notes: Although the flowers of woolly plantain are inconspicuous, the flower spikes of this common small annual are noticeable when they grow in masses along highways. The whole plant is densely covered with woolly white hairs, but it looks greenish from a distance. Indigenous Peoples have used a tea brewed from the plant as an appetite suppressant and have used it to treat headaches and diarrhea. It is sometimes called Indian wheat because the seeds were once harvested for food. The seeds are also eaten by birds and small rodents. This plant is widespread across the United States.

CLUSTER TYPE
Spike

FLOWER TYPE
Regular

LEAF TYPE
Simple

LEAF ATTACHMENT
Basal

dried
stems

Dune Evening-primrose
Oenothera deltoides

Family: Evening-primrose (Onagraceae)

Height: ½–3½' (15–107 cm)

Flower: saucer-shaped white (fading to pink) flowers, 1½–3½" (4–9 cm) wide, have 4 broad heart-shaped petals around a yellow center; sweetly fragrant

Leaf: pointed lance-shaped leaves, 1–6" (2.5–15 cm) long, hairy above; branching spreading stems, outer stems turn upward

Fruit: curved and twisted, cylindrical tan pod, ¾–2½" (2–6 cm) long

Bloom: Feb–May

Cycle/Origin: annual, perennial; native

Zone/Habitat: desert scrub below 3,000' (915 m); flats, dunes, among creosote bushes, sandy soils

Range: southwestern and northwestern corners of Arizona

Notes: After good winter rains, this wildflower is easily seen on the Mohawk Dunes (east of Yuma, Arizona) blooming in masses with desert sand verbena (pg. 167), covering large areas with color. As the plant dries, the outer stems curl upward and inward, forming a long-lasting structure reminiscent of old-fashioned wicker birdcages (see inset), thus it's also called birdcage evening-primrose. The species name *deltoides* is derived from the triangular-shaped Greek letter *delta* and refers to the shape of the petals.

FLOWER TYPE | LEAF TYPE | LEAF ATTACHMENT | FRUIT
Regular | **Simple** | **Alternate** | **Pod**

Doubting Mariposa Lily
Calochortus ambiguus

Family: Lily (Liliaceae)

Height: 12–24" (30–61 cm)

Flower: tulip-shaped white flower, 2" (5 cm) wide, has 3 large petals, each with fringed blotch at the base; 3 pointed oval pinkish sepals; dark-pink center

Leaf: grass-like basal leaves, 2–3" (5–7.5 cm) long, have a lengthwise groove; only a few smaller stem leaves; basal leaves wither before the plant blooms

Fruit: erect, narrowly oblong, brown capsule, 1½" (4 cm) long, 3-angled, has a pointed tip, contains flat seeds

Bloom: Apr–Aug

Cycle/Origin: perennial; native

Zone/Habitat: grasslands, interior chaparral, montane at 3,000–8,000' (915–2,440 m), slopes, open pine forests

Range: two-thirds of Arizona, in a wide band from the northwestern to southeastern corners of the state

Notes: This species is the most common of the five *Calochortus* lilies in Arizona. An erect bloom, it is also the most variable in flower color, ranging from white to purple and with variations in the dark-purple markings on the bases of the petals; it may even lack the dark markings altogether. The genus name *Calochortus* means "beautiful grass" in Greek and refers to the narrow grass-like leaves. Indigenous Peoples have roasted and eaten the bulbs of mariposa lilies.

FLOWER TYPE LEAF TYPE LEAF ATTACHMENT FRUIT
Regular **Simple** **Alternate** **Pod**

Fragrant Snakeroot
Ageratina herbacea

Family: Aster (Asteraceae)

Height: 12–24" (30–61 cm)

Flower: open flat cluster, 2" (5 cm) wide, of white flower heads, ⅜" 0(.9 cm) wide; each bloom is made up of tiny star-shaped tubular flowers (disk flowers) with long white male flower parts (stamens)

Leaf: triangular or lance-shaped, yellowish or grayish-green leaves, 1–3" (2.5–7.5 cm) long, have toothed edges and prominent veins

Bloom: Jun–Oct

Cycle/Origin: perennial; native

Zone/Habitat: oak/pinyon pine/juniper woodlands, montane at 5,000–9,000' (1,525–2,745 m); openings in ponderosa pine forests, along rocky streams, slopes, ridges, arroyos

Range: throughout, except the southwestern corner

Notes: This common mountain perennial with white flower clusters attracts many species of butterflies and other insects. The whole plant is fragrant when dried. Woody underground stems (rhizomes), thought to resemble snakes, account for "snakeroot" in the common name. The Navajo have used an infusion of the leaves as a tea and applied it as a lotion to treat fever and headaches.

CLUSTER TYPE
Flat

FLOWER TYPE
Composite

LEAF TYPE
Simple

LEAF ATTACHMENT
Opposite

Common Yarrow
Achillea millefolium

Family: Aster (Asteraceae)

Height: 12–36" (30–91 cm)

Flower: flat cluster, 2–4" (5–10 cm) wide, of 5–20 densely packed, white (sometimes pink) flower heads; each small flower head, ¼" (0.6 cm) wide, of 4–6 (usually 5) petals surrounding a tiny center

Leaf: fern-like, finely divided, feathery leaves, 4–6" (10–15 cm) long, have a strong aroma and become progressively smaller toward the top of the hairy stem; stalked lower and stalkless upper leaves

Bloom: Mar–Nov

Cycle/Origin: perennial; native

Zone/Habitat: all life zones above 4,500' (1,370 m); pine forest openings, fields, disturbed sites, along roads

Range: throughout

Notes: It's a common wildflower of open fields and along roads. A native of Eurasia, as well as North America, common yarrows are probably native in Arizona since the Zuni people have used the plant in rituals. Often confused with a type of fern because of its leaves, it grows in large clusters due to a horizontal underground stem. *Achillea* comes from the Greek legend that Achilles used the plant to treat bleeding wounds during the Trojan War. *Millefolium* means "thousand leaves," referring to the many divisions of the leaf, making one leaf look like many.

CLUSTER TYPE
Flat

FLOWER TYPE
Composite

LEAF TYPE
Simple Lobed

LEAF ATTACHMENT
Alternate

273

Narrowleaf Popcornflower

Johnstonella angustifolia

Family: Forget-me-not (Boraginaceae)

Height: 3–18" (7.5–45 cm)

Flower: coiled spike cluster, 2–5" (5–13 cm) long, of tiny white flowers; each tubular flower made of 5 fused petals held by a very fuzzy green bract

Leaf: narrowly lance-shaped or oblong basal leaves, ½–1½" (1–4 cm) long, are grayish green, opposite or alternate; leaves and stems densely covered with stiff, bristly white hairs

Bloom: Feb–Jun

Cycle/Origin: annual; native

Zone/Habitat: 512–8,500' (160–2,591 m), from deserts to the pine belt

Range: all over Arizona

Notes: Previously the plants of this genus were called *Cryptantha* (Greek for "hidden flower") because the individual flowers are very small. Often the more than 35 species in Arizona can only be distinguished from each other with a floral key and a microscope. This low-growing species is also called desert popcornflower because it is widespread and abundant in deserts, a benefit to the slow-moving desert tortoises that eat this very fuzzy plant. Although popcornflowers (*Johnstonella* spp.) are in the same family and share their common name with the much-less-hairy Arizona popcornflower (pg. 259), they are not closely related.

CLUSTER TYPE
Spike

FLOWER TYPE
Tube

LEAF TYPE
Simple

LEAF ATTACHMENT
Alternate

LEAF ATTACHMENT
Opposite

fruit

Red Whisker Clammyweed
Polanisia dodecandra

Family: Spiderflower (Cleomaceae)

Height: 12–36" (30–91 cm)

Flower: elongated flower clusters, 2–6" (5–15 cm) long, of frilly, pinkish-white flowers; each bloom, ¾" (2 cm) wide, has 4 clawed petals notched at tips, many protruding pinkish-purple flower parts

Leaf: stalked, dark-green leaves, 2½–4" (6–10 cm) long, are clammy to the touch and divided into 3 fine-haired elliptical leaflets; upper leaves are smaller

Fruit: bean-like, reddish-green pod, 1–3" (2.5–7.5 cm) long, is erect, flattened, and fuzzy; turns tan

Bloom: May–Oct

Cycle/Origin: annual; native

Zone/Habitat: desert scrub at 1,000–6,500' (305–1,980 m); along roads and washes, disturbed areas, banks of streams

Range: wide band down the center of Arizona, from the northern to southern borders

Notes: The foliage of this sticky-haired annual has a rank resinous odor and so many glands on its surface that it feels chilly and moist, thus the name "clammyweed." *Dodecandra* means "having 12 stamens" in Latin, referring to the long obvious flower parts. Often cultivated for the scentless airy flowers, it self-sows readily, filling in empty spots in the garden. It grows best in full sun.

CLUSTER TYPE	FLOWER TYPE	LEAF TYPE	LEAF ATTACHMENT	FRUIT
Round	**Irregular**	**Palmate**	**Alternate**	**Pod**

flower

fruit

Spider Milkweed
Asclepias asperula

Family: Dogbane (Apocynaceae)

Height: 8–24" (20–61 cm)

Flower: round clusters, 3" (7.5 cm) wide, of greenish-white flowers tinged with purple; each bloom, ½" (1 cm) wide, has 5 upward-curving petals and a 5-part crown of purple horns tipped with white

Leaf: narrow triangular leaves, 4–6" (10–15 cm) long, are dark green with a grayish middle vein and have pointed tips and wavy edges that curl upward

Fruit: stout curved conical pod, 6" (15 cm) long, is green with pink streaks and has deep lengthwise wrinkles and a pointed tip; contains flat brown seeds

Bloom: Apr–Aug

Cycle/Origin: perennial; native

Zone/Habitat: desert scrub, oak/pinyon pine/juniper woodlands, and montane at 3,000–9,000' (915–2,745 m); flats, slopes, along sandy washes, openings among trees

Range: throughout, except the southwestern corner

Notes: Pairs of conical pods resemble the curved horns of the pronghorn antelope, thus it is also called antelope horns. Inside the pod, teardrop-shaped seeds are in spiral layers around hair-like white fuzz that carries the seeds away on the wind. The foliage, which contains alkaloids, is eaten by monarch butterfly caterpillars, rendering them and their resulting butterflies poisonous to predators.

CLUSTER TYPE
Round

FLOWER TYPE
Irregular

LEAF TYPE
Simple

LEAF ATTACHMENT
Alternate

FRUIT
Pod

fruit

Southwestern Prickly Poppy
Argemone pleiacantha

Family: Poppy (Papaveraceae)

Height: 1½–4' (45–122 cm)

Flower: slightly cupped white flowers with bright-yellowish-orange centers; each flower, 3–5" (7.5–13 cm) wide, has 4–6 wrinkled, paper-thin, overlapping petals

Leaf: lance-shaped, bluish-green leaves, 2–8" (5–20 cm) long, have spine-tipped deep lobes; spiny stem

Fruit: oblong erect green pod, 1–2" (2.5–5 cm) long, turns brown; bumpy, spiny, and has many tiny dark seeds

Bloom: middle Mar–Nov

Cycle/Origin: annual, perennial; native

Zone/Habitat: desert scrub, grasslands, oak/pinyon pine/juniper woodlands at 500–7,000' (150–2,135 m); mesas, along washes

Range: throughout

Notes: The white petals surrounding the orange center give rise to another common name for this plant, cowboy's fried egg. It grows abundantly in overgrazed or otherwise disturbed soils such as along highways. The entire plant is poisonous due to the numerous toxic alkaloids it contains, although mourning doves do eat the seeds. The stem sap is yellow and foul smelling, but the flowers are fragrant and attract bees and moths. Interestingly, butterflies usually do not visit this poppy.

FLOWER TYPE
Regular

LEAF TYPE
Simple Lobed

LEAF ATTACHMENT
Alternate

LEAF ATTACHMENT
Clasping

FRUIT
Pod

fruit

False Solomon's Seal

Maianthemum racemosum

Family: Asparagus (Asparagaceae)

Height: 12–36" (30–91 cm)

Flower: spike cluster, 3–5" (7.5–13 cm) long, of tiny star-shaped white flowers, at end of single long arching stem; each flower, 1/8" (.3 cm) wide, has 3 petals and 3 petal-like sepals, giving the appearance of 6 petals

Leaf: stalkless elliptical leaves, 3–6" (7.5–15 cm) long, heavy parallel veining above, finely hairy below

Fruit: clusters of waxy green berries with red speckles, each berry, 1/4" (.6 cm) wide, turns translucent red

Bloom: May–Jul

Cycle/Origin: perennial; native

Zone/Habitat: montane and subalpine at 6,000–10,000' (1,830–3,050 m), coniferous forests, moist soils

Range: northeastern two-thirds and southeastern corner of Arizona

Notes: The dense spike flower cluster at the end of the arching stem and the red berries are characteristic of this plant. It grows on forest floors from an elongated horizontal underground stem. Historically, the waxy berries were eaten and the plant was cultivated. A round scar on the stem (left after the stem has broken off) resembles the seal of King Solomon, hence the reference in the common name. Also called Solomon's plume for its feather-like flower spike.

CLUSTER TYPE **Spike**   FLOWER TYPE **Regular**   LEAF TYPE **Simple**   LEAF ATTACHMENT **Alternate**   FRUIT **Berry**

Western White Clematis
Clematis ligusticifolia

Family: Buttercup (Ranunculaceae)

Height: 9–18' (2.7–5.5 m); vine

Flower: flat, dense, white or cream cluster, 3–8" (7.5–20 cm) wide, of 7–20 flowers, 1" (2.5 cm) wide; has 4 white petal-like sepals around erect white flower parts

Leaf: smooth, stalked, dark-green leaves divided into 5–7 irregularly toothed or lobed leaflets that are 1–3½" (2.5–9 cm) long; leaves oppositely attached

Fruit: fuzzy ball-shaped green fruit, 1½–2" (4–5 cm) wide; contains a single seed with many long silky hairs; fruit bursts when ripe, releasing the fluff and seed

Bloom: May–Sep

Cycle/Origin: perennial, native

Zone/Habitat: interior chaparral, oak/pinyon pine/juniper woods, riparian deciduous, montane at 3,000–8,000' (915–2,440 m); climbing in trees, on fences, near seeps

Range: eastern two-thirds of Arizona

Notes: This woody vine forms dense clinging mats high in shrubs or trees. In the female plants, the flowers are followed by large white or yellow plumes of fluff and seeds, thus another common name, old man's beard. This fluff makes excellent tinder for starting fires and has been used as insulation in footwear and to soak up moisture in babies' diapers. An extract made from the peppery leaves has been used by Indigenous Peoples to treat colds and skin sores.

CLUSTER TYPE
Flat

FLOWER TYPE
Regular

LEAF TYPE
Compound

LEAF ATTACHMENT
Opposite

FRUIT
Pod

Tufted Evening-primrose
Oenothera cespitosa

Family: Evening-primrose (Onagraceae)

Height: 2–8" (5–20 cm)

Flower: white flower, turning pinkish white, 4" (10 cm) wide, with 4 wide heart-shaped petals and 4 long, thin, pointed pink sepals that curve downward

Leaf: lance-shaped to narrowly elliptical basal leaves, 2–8" (5–20 cm) long, have irregular teeth or are lobed

Fruit: cylindrical brown capsule, turning woody, ½–3" (1–7.5 cm) long, is hairy, knobby, and angled

Bloom: Apr–Sep

Cycle/Origin: perennial; native

Zone/Habitat: desert scrub, grasslands, interior chaparral and oak/pinyon pine/juniper woodlands at 3,000–7,500' (915–2,285 m); on rocky slopes, among ponderosa pines

Range: throughout

Notes: Like other evening-primroses, this fragrant flower opens in late afternoon, blooms through the night, and closes by the next morning. It's pollinated by hawk moths, which are attracted by the white color and the scent of the flowers. It is evergreen in most habitats, but the foliage does turn red and drops off in cold conditions. A lovely addition to gardens in extremely dry habitats, it likes well-drained soil and tolerates heat. Give it a little water weekly, and it will produce new blooms over a long period of time.

FLOWER TYPE
Regular

LEAF TYPE
Simple

LEAF TYPE
Simple Lobed

LEAF ATTACHMENT
Alternate

FRUIT
Pod

287

Desert Lily
Hesperocallis undulata

Family: Asparagus (Asparagaceae)

Height: 1–4' (30–122 cm)

Flower: loose spike cluster, 4–12" (10–30 cm) long, of large trumpet-shaped white flowers, 3" (7.5 cm) long; each bloom has 6 waxy, long oval petals with a greenish-silver streak on the back, flaring widely around protruding yellow-tipped flower parts

Leaf: bluish-green, long, narrow, basal blades, 8–20" (20–50 cm) long, partially folded down their centers, smooth wavy edges; a few smaller stem leaves

Fruit: tan pod, ½" (1 cm) long

Bloom: middle Feb–May, following rain

Cycle/Origin: perennial; native

Zone/Habitat: desert scrub below 2,500' (760 m); sand dunes, flats, rocky hills, mesas, among creosote bushes

Range: western third of Arizona

Notes: This sweetly fragrant flower looks similar to the cultivated Easter lily. Genetic studies have shown it is actually more closely related to succulent yuccas and agaves, thus it was reclassified from the Lily family to the Asparagus family. In spring, it can be seen at the edges of sand dunes by the airbase near Yuma, Arizona. It's also called ajo lily for the garlic-flavored bulbs, which have been dug up and eaten by Indigenous Peoples and early Spanish settlers (*ajo* is Spanish for "garlic"). The deeply buried bulbs can remain dormant for years, awaiting enough moisture to grow.

CLUSTER TYPE	FLOWER TYPE	LEAF TYPE	LEAF ATTACHMENT	FRUIT
Spike	**Tube**	**Simple**	**Basal**	**Pod**

fruit

Sacred Datura
Datura wrightii

Family: Nightshade (Solanaceae)

Height: 1–5' (30–152 cm)

Flower: trumpet-shaped white (sometimes tinged with lavender) flower, 6–8" (15–20 cm) long, has 5 large fused petals with slightly wavy outer ends and a short spike at the middle edge of each petal

Leaf: arrowhead-shaped leaves, 1–10" (2.5–25 cm) long, are dark bluish green and have prominent veins

Fruit: globular prickly green pod, turns brown at maturity, 1½" (4 cm) wide

Bloom: Apr–Nov

Cycle/Origin: perennial; native

Zone/Habitat: desert scrub at 100–6,500' (30–1,980 m); mesas, along roads and washes, disturbed areas

Range: throughout

Notes: The fragrant flowers of sacred datura, which are pollinated by hawk moths, open in the evening and wither a few hours after sunrise. All parts contain hallucinogenic compounds and are poisonous—just handling the plant can cause skin irritation. Daturas have been important to Indigenous Peoples, who have used them for medicinal and ritual purposes, thus "sacred" in the common name. It's also called sacred thornapple for the seedpod, which resembles a spiny apple. It's one of five species in the *Datura* genus in Arizona.

FLOWER TYPE	LEAF TYPE	LEAF ATTACHMENT	LEAF ATTACHMENT	FRUIT
Tube	**Simple**	**Alternate**	**Opposite**	**Pod**

Foothill Deervetch

Acmispon brachycarpus

Family: Pea or Bean (Fabaceae)

Height: 2–4" (5–10 cm)

Flower: tiny pea-like yellow flowers, ⅛" (.3 cm) long, turning red with age

Leaf: very hairy leaves, ½" (1 cm) long, are palmate, divided into 4 tiny oval leaflets with pointed tips

Fruit: erect oblong tan pod, ½" (1 cm) long

Bloom: Mar–Jun

Cycle/Origin: annual; native

Zone/Habitat: desert scrub, grasslands, oak/pinyon pine/juniper woodlands below 5,500' (1,675 m); rocky slopes, flats, along roads

Range: two-thirds of Arizona, in a wide band from the northwestern to southeastern corners of the state

Notes: A very common plant in deserts and grasslands, foothill deervetch forms dense, low-growing mats made up of hairy, succulent-looking small leaves and even tinier flowers. It is now more often being used in landscaping, as it makes a good ground cover. This nutritious member of the Pea and Bean family is vital to the desert tortoise—the leaves comprise a third of the tortoise's spring diet. Exotic nonnative plants that crowd out native species are not eaten by desert tortoises and threaten their survival. The seeds are one of the main foods that Gambel's quail and scaled quail eat year-round.

FLOWER TYPE   LEAF TYPE   LEAF ATTACHMENT   FRUIT
Irregular   **Palmate**   **Alternate**   **Pod**

Many-bristled Cinchweed
Pectis papposa

Family: Aster (Asteraceae)

Height: 4–10" (10–25 cm)

Flower: small yellow flower head, ¼–½" (.6–1 cm) wide, is daisy-like and made up of 8 pointed petals (ray flowers) around a small yellow center; groups of blossoms loosely arranged at tops of sticky stems

Leaf: thread-like, dark-green leaves, ½–2½" (1–6 cm) long, several pairs of bristles and sticky glands on the edges; oppositely attached to low-branching stem

Bloom: Jul–Nov, but only after summer monsoons

Cycle/Origin: annual; native

Zone/Habitat: desert scrub below 5,000' (1,525 m); flats, along roads, sandy dunes, rocky slopes

Range: throughout Arizona, except the northeastern corner of the state

Notes: This plant forms low mounds covered with loose clusters of yellow composite blooms. Found in most of the Southwest, it flowers only after summer rains. In good years it can dominate the landscape, covering large expanses of desert. It's the only annual that blooms in the summer in the Mojave Desert, where rain rarely falls during that season. This flower is common in the Cabeza Prieta National Wildlife Refuge of southwestern Arizona, which has over 1,000 square miles (385 sq. km) of wilderness.

FLOWER TYPE   LEAF TYPE   LEAF ATTACHMENT
Composite   **Simple**   **Opposite**

295

Greenleaf Five Eyes
Chamaesaracha coronopus

Family: Nightshade (Solanaceae)

Height: 6–18" (15–45 cm)

Flower: star-shaped flower of pale greenish yellow to cream, ⅓–¾" (.8–2 cm) wide, of fused fuzzy sepals and petals held by globe-shaped green calyx; each petal has a raised yellow or white spot at the base

Leaf: narrowly lance-shaped leaves, 1–4" (2.5–10 cm) long, are thick and rough, hairy with wavy margins

Fruit: berry-like yellowish fruit, ¼" (.6 cm) wide, has dark-brown seeds; persistent 5-lobed papery calyx

Bloom: Apr–Sep

Cycle/Origin: perennial; native

Zone/Habitat: desert scrub, grasslands, interior chaparral, pinyon pine/juniper woods at 2,500–7,500' (760–2,285 m); abandoned fields, mesas, plains

Range: scattered locations throughout Arizona, but mostly in the northern and central parts of the state

Notes: This low-growing plant is also called small groundcherry or prostrate groundcherry for its yellow fruit and sprawling stems. The mounded yellow or white spot at the base of each narrow petal gives rise to "five eyes" in the common name. It's different from the closely related velvet hairy five eyes (*C. sordida*) (not shown), which lacks spots on its petals and is found only near water.

FLOWER TYPE	LEAF TYPE	LEAF ATTACHMENT	FRUIT
Regular	**Simple**	**Alternate**	**Berry**

Woolly Cinquefoil
Potentilla hippiana

Family: Rose (Rosaceae)

Height: 3–20" (7.6–50 cm)

Flower: lemon-yellow, simple blossom, ½" (1.3 cm) wide, has 5 shallowly notched, broadly heart-shaped yellow petals with orange at the tapered centers, backed by green triangular sepals showing between the petals

Leaf: feather-shaped, deep-green leaves, 2–6" (5–15 cm) long, are silver below, with 3–6 pairs of deeply divided leaflets arranged ladder-like, each lobe coarsely toothed and edges curl upward; mostly basal leaves attached on long stalks (petioles)

Bloom: Jun–Aug

Cycle/Origin: perennial; native

Zone/Habitat: mountain meadows and aspen, ponderosa pine or mixed conifer woodlands at 6,500–11,500' (1,980–3,510 m)

Range: northeastern and southeastern corners, about half of Arizona, but especially along the Mogollon Rim

Notes: Unlike other plants in the genus *Potentilla*, most of which have five-fingered or palmate leaves, this variable species has leaves broadly in the shape of a feather, but with wide leaflets that have very definite teeth along all the margins. More than 20 species of *Potentilla* occur in Arizona, with mostly similar yellow flowers. Ground-hugging, it can be used as an attractive ground-cover in higher-elevation gardens.

FLOWER TYPE
Regular

LEAF TYPE
Compound

LEAF ATTACHMENT
Alternate

LEAF ATTACHMENT
Basal

fruit

Slender Janusia
Cottsia gracilis

Family: Malpighia (Malpighiaceae)

Height: 6–9' (1.8–2.7 m); vine

Flower: lemon-yellow flowers, ½" (1 cm) wide, have 5 wrinkled spoon-shaped petals around a green center

Leaf: narrowly lance-shaped leaves, ½–1½" (1–4 cm) long, are green, hairy above and below, and oppositely attached along slender twining grayish stems

Fruit: reddish seedpods, 1" (2.5 cm) wide, with 2–3 flat thin wings, fuzzy with white hairs

Bloom: Apr–Oct

Cycle/Origin: perennial; native

Zone/Habitat: desert scrub at 1,000–5,000' (305–1,525 m); along roads and washes, flats, rocky slopes

Range: southern half and northwestern corner of Arizona

Notes: Aptly named *gracilis* for its graceful appearance, this slender, twining, climbing vine grows on and becomes entangled with cacti, desert trees, and shrubs. The odd flowers with their paddle-shaped petals are soon followed by the fuzzy winged red seedpods. Vegetarian desert tortoises feed on the foliage and pods. This short-lived perennial grows only in small areas of southwestern New Mexico and Texas, although it is widespread in Arizona and northern Mexico. Slender janusia can be easily found along the roadways in Saguaro National Park, located west of Tucson.

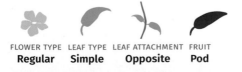

FLOWER TYPE	LEAF TYPE	LEAF ATTACHMENT	FRUIT
Regular	**Simple**	**Opposite**	**Pod**

Wright Deervetch
Lotus wrightii

Family: Pea or Bean (Fabaceae)

Height: 8–16" (20–40 cm)

Flower: pea-like yellow flower, ½" (1 cm) long, turning orange or red; upper petal (standard) is rust colored below and flares backward

Leaf: dark-green leaves, divided into 3–5 oblong narrow leaflets of differing sizes from ¼–½" (.6–1 cm) long; trailing, reclining stem; leaves turn red in autumn

Fruit: bean-like, greenish-red pod, turning brown, ⅝–1" (1.5–2.5 cm) long, is slender and flattened

Bloom: Apr–Sep

Cycle/Origin: perennial; native

Zone/Habitat: oak/pinyon pine/juniper woods, riparian decid-uous montane at 4,500–9,000' (1,370–2,745 m); among ponderosa pines, canyons, meadows

Range: throughout, except the southwestern corner

Notes: This upright or trailing, vine-like plant has conspicuous bright-yellow blooms and is often found along streams in canyons. There are several stems arising from the base, but the stems have very few branches. It's slow-growing and tolerant of dry or cold conditions. It sheds its leaves in the winter, dying back to the ground, and grows from the root in the spring. Fire-adapted, Wright deervetch actually increases in abundance following high-intensity fires, which have been occurring more frequently in the Southwest.

FLOWER TYPE
Irregular

LEAF TYPE
Compound

LEAF ATTACHMENT
Alternate

FRUIT
Pod

Many-flowered Puccoon

Lithospermum multiflorum

Family: Forget-me-not (Boraginaceae)

Height: 6–24" (15–61 cm)

Flower: groups of 2–10 trumpet-shaped, drooping yellow flowers; each flower, ½" (1 cm) wide, has a wide mouth with 5 rounded lobes; base of the flower is clasped by 5 slender, pointed hairy bracts

Leaf: bluish-green leaves, 1–2½" (2.5–6 cm) long, are long, thin, and hairy with margins rolled under; upper leaves are gradually smaller; 2–3 small bracts at each leaf attachment (axis); hairy single stem

Bloom: Jun–Sep

Cycle/Origin: perennial; native

Zone/Habitat: pinyon pine/juniper woodlands, montane and subalpine at 6,000–9,500' (1,830–2,895 m); on slopes, along streams, limestone soils

Range: northern half and southeastern corner of Arizona

Notes: Often found under ponderosa pines, this hairy, erect plant has a single slender stem topped with a group of yellow tubular flowers. The genus name *Lithospermum* is from the words for "stone" and "seed," referring to the very hard, ripe nutlets that look like tiny polished stones. These stony nutlets have been eaten by Indigenous Peoples. The root has been used for medicinal purposes and as a purple dye. In fact, "puccoon" in the common name is an Algonquian word referring to plants that yield dyes.

FLOWER TYPE **Tube**   LEAF TYPE **Simple**   LEAF ATTACHMENT **Alternate**

leaves

Dogweed
Thymophylla pentachaeta

Family: Aster (Asteraceae)

Height: 4–8" (10–20 cm)

Flower: small, daisy-like, yellow flower head, ½" (1 cm) wide, has 12–21 (usually 13) short oval petals around a wide, orangish-yellow center of many tiny disk flowers; each bloom on its own, nearly leafless stalk well above the leaves

Leaf: stiffly lobed, sticky, slightly fuzzy leaves, 1" (2.5 cm) long, divided into 3–5 (usually 5) thread-like lobes with pointed prickly tips; leaves on lower half of the stem only; the plant has many densely leafy stems

Bloom: Mar–Sep

Cycle/Origin: perennial; native

Zone/Habitat: desert scrub at 2,500–4,500' (760–1,370 m); on flats, slopes, roadsides

Range: throughout Arizona, except the southwestern and northeastern corners of the state

Notes: This very common, low-growing perennial is found on desert flats and often seen growing along roadways and in natural areas of Tucson. The individual small flower heads are inconspicuous, but a yellow haze appears to float above the desert floor after heavy rains, when mats of dogweed bloom. The aromatic leaves are required food for the caterpillars of the tiny dainty sulphur butterfly. It's also called five-needle pricklyleaf for the needle-like lobes of the leaves.

FLOWER TYPE
Composite

LEAF TYPE
Simple Lobed

LEAF ATTACHMENT
Opposite

Sweetbush
Bebbia juncea

Family: Aster (Asteraceae)

Height: 1–4' (30–122 cm); shrub

Flower: button-like, yellow flower head, ½" (1 cm) wide, is rayless, made up of tiny disk flowers only and clasped by fuzzy, pointed, whitish-green bracts with tips that curl downward; leafless fuzzy flower stalk

Leaf: few lance-shaped leaves, ½–1" (1–2.5 cm) long, have smooth edges (sometimes lobed) with pointed tips, are rough and hairy, oppositely attached to hairy stems; leaves fall off in times of drought

Bloom: Apr–Jul

Cycle/Origin: perennial; native

Zone/Habitat: desert scrub below 4,000' (1,220 m); rocky slopes, among creosote bushes, flats, plateaus, along washes

Range: throughout Arizona, except northeastern corner

Notes: This densely branched shrub forms a naturally rounded bush that is leafless most of the year. The thin green stems continue to make food (photosynthesis) during dry periods when leafless and have fuzzy white hairs that decrease the evaporation of water from the pores on their surface. The yellow blooms of this perennial are never numerous enough to obscure the green branches. It's also called chuckwalla's delight, as the plant is a favorite food of the chuckwalla, a large native vegetarian lizard.

FLOWER TYPE   LEAF TYPE   LEAF ATTACHMENT
Composite   **Simple**   **Opposite**

American Threefold
Trixis californica

Family: Aster (Asteraceae)

Height: 12–36" (30–91 cm); shrub

Flower: yellow flower head, ½–¾" (1–2 cm) wide, that appears to have petals (ray flowers) but actually has 9–15 tubular disk flowers flaring out into two yellow lips; lower lip is petal-like and upper lip is tightly coiled backward; conspicuous male flower parts (anthers) protrude well above each disk flower

Leaf: narrowly lance-shaped, yellowish-green leaves, 1–2" (2.5–5 cm) long, are evergreen, rigid, have margins rolled under and winged leafstalks; leafy stiff stems

Bloom: Feb–Oct, mostly in spring, but anytime after rain

Cycle/Origin: perennial; native

Zone/Habitat: desert scrub, grasslands, oak/pinyon pine woodlands below 5,500' (1,675 m); gravel slopes, flats

Range: throughout Arizona, except northeastern corner

Notes: The unique fragrant flower heads appear to have ray flowers around the center like other asters, but the petals are actually the extended outer lip of the tubular disk flowers. The many dense, foul-smelling leaves get progressively smaller up the stem to just under the blooms. It's also called plumilla, Spanish for "little feather," for the tufts of golden bristles on its seed-like fruit. The Seri Indians, who live along the Gulf of California, believe this plant has important medicinal properties.

FLOWER TYPE
Composite

LEAF TYPE
Simple

LEAF ATTACHMENT
Alternate

LEAF ATTACHMENT
Whorl

Camphorweed

Heterotheca subaxillaris

Family: Aster (Asteraceae)

Height: 1–5' (30–152 cm)

Flower: daisy-like yellow flower head, ½–1" (1–2.5 cm) wide, composed of 15–30 petals (ray flowers) and a yellow-orange center (disk flowers); many flower heads per plant atop the branched upper stem

Leaf: oval leaves, 1–4" (2.5–10 cm) long, have smooth or slightly toothed margins, are stalked and alternate lower on the stem; leaves along middle and upper stem are stalkless and clasping; leaves and the single stem are hairy and sticky due to glands in the hairs

Bloom: Mar–Nov

Cycle/Origin: annual, biennial; native

Zone/Habitat: desert scrub and grasslands at 1,000–5,500' (305–1,525 m); along roads, disturbed sites, open areas, old fields, dunes

Range: central and southeastern Arizona

Notes: This sparsely or densely leaved aster is named for the camphor-like odor emitted from its leaves when crushed. It is very weedy and drought tolerant. Ranchers dislike it because cows avoid eating it, and the plant can overtake pastures. However, it does serve as food for the caterpillars of several moth species. When applied to injuries, such as sprains or bruises, the foliage is said to diminish pain, inflammation, and swelling.

FLOWER TYPE **Composite** LEAF TYPE **Simple** LEAF ATTACHMENT **Alternate** LEAF ATTACHMENT **Clasping**

Burroweed
Isocoma tenuisecta

Family: Aster (Asteraceae)

Height: 12–36" (30–91 cm); shrub

Flower: round clusters, ½–1" (1–2.5 cm) wide, of tiny, disk-shaped, daisy-like, golden-yellow flower heads at tips of woody stems; each bloom has only disk flowers (no ray flowers)

Leaf: stiffly upright, sticky, dark-green leaves, 1–1½" (2.5–4 cm) long, are deeply divided into 4–8 short slim lobes with sharply pointed tips

Bloom: Sep–Nov

Cycle/Origin: perennial; native

Zone/Habitat: desert scrub, grasslands, oak/pinyon pine/juniper woodlands at 2,000–6,500' (610–1,980 m); dry slopes, along roads, disturbed areas, scattered on rangelands, among creosote bushes

Range: southeastern two-thirds of Arizona, especially around Tucson

Notes: It forms rounded, semi-woody bushes topped with yellow blooms that turn tan when dry and remain on the plant. It's becoming common in landscaping. The foliage is toxic if eaten by livestock, particularly horses. Cows grazing on burroweed produce milk containing tremetol, a chemical poisonous to people. It will become invasive in overgrazed pastures. It occurs in the wild only in Arizona and New Mexico in the US and in northern Mexico.

CLUSTER TYPE
Round

FLOWER TYPE
Composite

LEAF TYPE
Simple Lobed

LEAF ATTACHMENT
Alternate

Seep Monkeyflower
Erythranthe guttata

Family: Monkeyflower (Phrymaceae)

Height: 2–36" (5–91 cm)

Flower: loose groups of vivid-yellow flowers; each tubular flower, ⅜–1½" (.9–4 cm) long, has erect upper 2-lobed petal (lip) and 3-lobed lower lip; swollen, hairy, red-spotted patches nearly close the throat

Leaf: fleshy, dark-green leaves, ½–4" (1–10 cm) long, are round and coarsely toothed; upper leaves are much smaller and stalkless; fleshy-walled stems are hollow

Fruit: oval brown pod, ½" (1 cm) long, thickest in the middle, tapering at both ends

Bloom: Mar–Sep

Cycle/Origin: annual, perennial; native

Zone/Habitat: riparian deciduous in all life zones at 500–9,500' (150–2,895 m); seeps, along washes, streambeds

Range: throughout

Notes: This plant can be tall and spindly, or short and bushy. It's mostly found on land at seeps, along streams or near springs, but it's sometimes found floating in water with its roots submerged. It will take advantage of the smallest bit of moist sand to grow at the bottom of a desert wash, surprising hikers with its vivid flowers. Native Americans have eaten the succulent leaves as salad greens. *Guttata* means "specks," referring to the red spots on the lower petals.

FLOWER TYPE **Irregular**   LEAF TYPE **Simple**   LEAF ATTACHMENT **Opposite**   FRUIT **Pod**

fruit

Gordon Bladderpod
Physaria gordonii

Family: Mustard (Brassicaceae)

Height: 4–16" (10–40 cm)

Flower: loose groups of bright-yellow flowers; each flower, ¾" (2 cm) wide, has 4 oval petals that are shallowly notched at the tips

Leaf: oblong or lance-shaped, grayish-green basal leaves, ½–3" (1–7.5 cm) long, variable margins; stem leaves are smaller, narrower; stems often lie on the ground

Fruit: nearly spherical, smooth green pod, ⅜" (.9 cm) wide, with a lengthwise brown band and tipped with thread-like projection; turns brown with age

Bloom: Feb–May

Cycle/Origin: annual, perennial, biennial; native

Zone/Habitat: desert scrub at 100–5,000' (30–1,525 m); on flats, along washes, slopes, under shrubs

Range: southernmost quarter of Arizona

Notes: In Arizona, this showy mustard is limited to only four counties in the south. After good winter rains, it occurs in huge patches on flats among creosote bushes. It's especially obvious and abundant in northeastern Tucson along the popular Catalina Highway, which goes up Mount Lemmon in the Santa Catalina Mountains. When stepped on, the seedpods make a popping sound, hence another common name, popweed. It ranges east to Texas and north to Kansas.

FLOWER TYPE **Regular**   LEAF TYPE **Simple**   LEAF TYPE **Simple Lobed**   LEAF ATTACHMENT **Alternate**   LEAF ATTACHMENT **Basal**   FRUIT **Pod**

California Suncup
Eulobus californicus

Family: Evening-primrose (Onagraceae)

Height: 2–4' (61–122 cm)

Flower: yellow flowers, ¾" (2 cm) wide, have 4 oval petals with red spots at the bases and protruding yellow flower parts

Leaf: narrowly elliptical, dark-green basal leaves, 2–6" (5–15 cm) long, have irregular pairs of sharp-pointed lobes; smaller stem leaves are sparse, narrower, and smooth edged or toothed

Fruit: orangish red seedpod, 2–4" (5–10 cm) long, is long and slender, 4-angled, and bends downward

Bloom: Feb–Jun

Cycle/Origin: annual, perennial; native

Zone/Habitat: desert scrub, grasslands, interior chaparral below 5,000' (1,525 m); along washes, slopes, roadsides

Range: western half of Arizona

Notes: This spindly wildflower has multibranched, smooth, erect, dark-green stems that bear a few scattered, bright-yellow flowers. The flowers open in the evening and close by the following midday. Although a member of the evening-primrose family, it resembles a mustard and is sometimes called mustard evening-primrose. This plant is so well adapted to wildfires in chaparral life zones that the seeds germinate best when first exposed to smoke.

FLOWER TYPE **Regular**　　LEAF TYPE **Simple**　　LEAF TYPE **Simple Lobed**　　LEAF ATTACHMENT **Alternate**　　LEAF ATTACHMENT **Basal**　　FRUIT **Pod**

fruit

Hoary Indian Mallow
Abutilon incanum

Family: Mallow (Malvaceae)

Height: 3–6' (.9–1.8 m)

Flower: orangish-yellow or white flowers, ¾" (2 cm) wide, have 5 broad petals around a yellow-and-red center

Leaf: elongated heart-shaped, velvety, grayish green leaves, ½–3" (1–7.5 cm) long, with scalloped or toothed edges and pointed tips; upper leaves much smaller or absent

Fruit: bowl-shaped dry yellow capsule, ½" (1 cm) wide, splits into 5 segments

Bloom: Mar–Oct

Cycle/Origin: perennial; native

Zone/Habitat: desert scrub at 1,000–4,500' (305–1,370 m); rocky flats, dry slopes, arroyos, along roads

Range: southern half and northwestern quarter of Arizona

Notes: This perennial is found in the Sonoran Desert in Arizona, but not in the Mojave Desert. The upright stems branch near the base and are less leafy higher up the stems. Like all plants in the Mallow family, the numerous male flower parts (stamens) are fused to form a central column, and the petals of the buds are twisted. The flowers of hoary Indian mallow can also be pink or white with round petals around a red center. It's also called sweet pelotazo.

FLOWER TYPE **Regular**   LEAF TYPE **Simple**   LEAF ATTACHMENT **Alternate**   FRUIT **Pod**

Shrubby Deervetch

Acmispon rigidus

Family: Pea or Bean (Fabaceae)

Height: 6–36" (15–91 cm)

Flower: pea-like yellow (sometimes orange-tinged) flower, ¾" (2 cm) long, upper petal (standard) flares backward and is rust-colored on the back; flower is clasped by hairy, reddish-green sepals (calyx); unopened buds are reddish orange

Leaf: leaves are alternate and widely spaced along several erect wiry stems; each leaf, ½–1" (1–2.5 cm) long, is divided into 3–4 oblong leaflets of uneven sizes

Fruit: narrow, straight, oblong smooth seedpod, ¾–1½" (2–4 cm) long, is green, turning reddish brown

Bloom: Feb–May

Cycle/Origin: perennial; native

Zone/Habitat: desert scrub, interior chaparral, pinyon pine/juniper woodlands at 200–5,500' (60–1,675 m); flats

Range: throughout Arizona, except the southeastern corner of the state

Notes: This upright, broom-like, wild pea frequently grows in soil that collects in boulder crevices. The species name *rigidus* and another common name, wiry lotus, describe the stiff wire-like stems that branch several times. With fewer leaves than other species of *Acmispon* in Arizona, it is better adapted to dry conditions, often blooming even during drought.

FLOWER TYPE	LEAF TYPE	LEAF ATTACHMENT	FRUIT
Irregular	**Palmate**	**Alternate**	**Pod**

325

Button Brittlebush
Encelia frutescens

Family: Aster (Asteraceae)

Height: 2–4' (61–122 cm); shrub

Flower: yellow-orange flower head, ¾" (2 cm) wide, is button-shaped, usually lacks petals (ray flowers), and has only tiny tubular yellow disk flowers; has protruding orange flower parts and white-haired green bracts; flower heads at tips of hairy stems

Leaf: oval, shiny, dark-green leaves, ½–1" (1–2.5 cm) long, have stiff hairs below and on wavy edges

Bloom: Feb–May and Aug–Sep, after rainfall

Cycle/Origin: perennial; native

Zone/Habitat: desert scrub below 4,000' (1,220 m); rocky slopes, mesas, flats, arroyos, roadsides

Range: throughout Arizona, except the southeastern corner

Notes: This plant is sometimes called green brittlebush for the color of the leaves, which can be distinguished from the bluish-green leaves of brittlebush (pg. 371). Aptly named *frutescens*, which means "shrubby" in Latin, this multibranched perennial has pinkish stems that turn whitish as they age. The solitary, disk-shaped flower heads tipping the stems have disk flowers and usually lack ray flowers, thus it is also called rayless encelia. This plant has been used by the Navajo and Kayenta tribes to treat shingles.

FLOWER TYPE LEAF TYPE LEAF ATTACHMENT
Composite **Simple** **Alternate**

Coves Cassia
Senna covesii

Family: Pea or Bean (Fabaceae)

Height: 12–24" (30–61 cm)

Flower: orangish-yellow flower, ¾–1½" (2–4 cm) wide, has 4 oblong, non-overlapping petals around a few dark flower parts; groups of 3–9 flowers, at end of a stalk from a leaf junction (axis), bloom a few at a time

Leaf: dark-bluish-green leaves, 2" (5 cm) long, divided into 2–3 pairs of elliptical short-stalked leaflets, ½–1" (1–2.5 cm) long; leafy stems have dense white hairs

Fruit: slightly curved, oblong green pod, ¾–2" (2–5 cm) long, turns woody

Bloom: Apr–Oct, especially after warm rains

Cycle/Origin: perennial; native

Zone/Habitat: desert scrub at 1,000–3,000' (305–915 m); slopes

Range: throughout, except the northwestern corner

Notes: It's also called desert senna for its habitat or rattlebox for the dry rattling sound the woody seedpods make when shaken. Bumblebees and carpenter bees pollinate the flowers by "buzz pollination"— bee lands on the flower and vibrates its flying muscles, causing the pollen to flow out of the anthers. The bee collects the pollen to eat later and inadvertently pollinates the next flower upon landing. It's an important food source for caterpillars of sleepy orange and cloudless sulphur butterflies. The Seri People of Mexico have used the root medicinally.

FLOWER TYPE
Regular

LEAF TYPE
Compound

LEAF ATTACHMENT
Alternate

FRUIT
Pod

Cutleaf Coneflower

Rudbeckia laciniata

Family: Aster (Asteraceae)

Height: 5–8' (1.5–2.4 m)

Flower: large yellow flower heads with narrow petals on tall stalks; each coneflower, ¾–5" (2–13 cm) wide, has a cone-shaped green center (disk flowers) surrounded by 8–12 drooping petals (ray flowers)

Leaf: lower leaves, 5–16" (13–40 cm) long, are divided into 3–7 sharp lobes with coarse teeth; upper leaves, 2–3" (5–7.5 cm) long, are simple, coarsely toothed, and nearly clasp the stem

Bloom: Jul–Sep

Cycle/Origin: perennial; native

Zone/Habitat: riparian deciduous, montane subalpine at 5,000–8,500' (1,525–2,590 m); meadows, along mountain streams, canyons, rich moist soils

Range: northern half and southeastern corner of Arizona

Notes: A tall and robust perennial, cutleaf coneflower grows in moist soils. Look for its green center (cone) and drooping yellow petals, along with the lobed lower leaves and simple upper leaves, to help identify it. It's often seen growing near streams, in meadows by coniferous forests, or in canyon bottoms. A good plant for a butterfly garden, its flowers attract butterflies such as monarchs, which drink the nectar. It's also known as green-headed coneflower or golden glow.

FLOWER TYPE
Composite

LEAF TYPE
Simple

LEAF TYPE
Simple Lobed

LEAF ATTACHMENT
Alternate

Flagstaff Ragwort
Senecio actinella

Family: Aster (Asteraceae)

Height: 3–16" (7–40 cm)

Flower: lemon-yellow, daisy-like flower, 1" (2.5 cm) wide, made up of 11–13 rectangular petals (ray flowers), with blunted tips around a yellow center and with a ring of white bristles at the base; a single composite flower tops each stem

Leaf: leathery, gray-green leaves, ¾–4" (2–10cm) long, are longer than wide and narrowest at their base, attached mainly near the base of the tall erect stems that can be densely hairy or smooth

Bloom: April–Sep

Cycle/Origin: perennial; native

Zone/Habitat: rocky, dry, ponderosa pine woodlands in mountains between 5,500–9,500' (1,700–2,900 m)

Range: found in southeastern corner and on a diagonal across the state, through the White Mountains

Notes: Tolerant of arid conditions, this plant can form large mats in ponderosa pine forest clearings because the perennial roots and some basal leaves remain throughout the year, sending up erect stems in spring to bloom from April through September. Senecio means old man or woman, referring to the white bristles at the base of the petals that are not visible unless you cut open the flower. Flagstaff ragwort is found in Arizona, New Mexico, and into Mexico. Commonly called butterweeds, there are more than 50 species of *Senecio* found in the western United States.

FLOWER TYPE   LEAF TYPE   LEAF ATTACHMENT   LEAF ATTACHMENT
Composite   Simple   Alternate   Basal

Whitestem Paperflower

Psilostrophe cooperi

Family: Aster (Asteraceae)

Height: 6–24" (15–61 cm); shrub

Flower: bright-yellow flower head, 1" (2.5 cm) wide, with 3–6 non-overlapping broad petals; each petal is tipped with 3 shallow lobes, folded at its base and appears inserted into the small yellow center

Leaf: narrowly lance-shaped, grayish-green leaves, ½–3½" (1–9 cm) long, have whitish hairs, pointed tips, and alternate along whitish stems; upper leaves smaller

Bloom: mostly Apr–Jun, but sometimes year-round

Cycle/Origin: perennial; native

Zone/Habitat: desert scrub, grasslands, oak/pinyon pine/juniper woods at 300–8,300' (90–2,530 m); along washes, among creosote bushes, plateaus, slopes

Range: throughout Arizona, except the northeastern and southwestern corners of the state

Notes: Whitestem paperflower is an open, branching shrub with matted, woolly-white hairs covering the stems. It forms a tangled, grayish-green mound that is covered with brilliant yellow when its flowers bloom. This common roadside wildflower is sometimes called paper daisy because the dried blooms, which remain on the plant for several weeks, look like daisies made of translucent tan paper. The dried flowers have been used in floral arrangements.

FLOWER TYPE **Composite** LEAF TYPE **Simple** LEAF ATTACHMENT **Alternate**

Lacy Tansy-aster
Xanthisma spinulosum

Family: Aster (Asteraceae)

Height: 8–24" (20–61 cm)

Flower: daisy-like, golden-yellow flower head, 1" (2.5 cm) wide, with layers of 30–45 narrow overlapping (can be non-overlapping) petals around an orangish-yellow center; clasped below by layers of pointed, bristle-tipped, erect bracts

Leaf: oblong to spoon-shaped, grayish-green leaves, ½–2½" (1–6 cm) long, are stalkless and have pairs of narrow lobes with smooth or toothed margins that are always tipped with bristly hairs; upper leaves tiny; thin woolly stems; branches are interwoven

Bloom: Feb–May

Cycle/Origin: perennial; native

Zone/Habitat: desert scrub, grasslands, oak/pinyon pine/juniper woodlands at 2,100–5,000' (640–1,525 m); in open areas

Range: throughout

Notes: Lacy tansy-aster leaves and flowers are highly variable. Look for the solitary, golden-yellow flowers that appear to float above the erect branches because the leaves are tiny on the upper stems. "Lacy" in the common name is for the feather-like leaves found on the lower half of the stems. It's also called cut-leaf iron plant for the lobed leaves and its woody base, which is very hard when dried.

FLOWER TYPE	LEAF TYPE	LEAF TYPE	LEAF ATTACHMENT
Composite	**Simple**	**Simple Lobed**	**Alternate**

leaves

Fineleaf Hymenopappus
Hymenopappus filifolius

Family: Aster (Asteraceae)

Height: 12–30" (30–76 cm)

Flower: golden-yellow flower heads, 1" (2.5 cm) wide, are round and spiky, on long thin leafless stalks; each blossom is made up of enlarged disk flowers only (no ray flowers) with protruding flower parts and is cupped by fuzzy whitish-green bracts

Leaf: grayish-green, woolly basal leaves, 3–8" (7.5–20 cm) long, are sticky, usually feather-like, and divided into thread-like lobes; can be simple and narrowly oval; sometimes a few much-smaller leaves along stem

Bloom: May–Sep

Cycle/Origin: perennial; native

Zone/Habitat: interior chaparral, oak/pinyon pine/juniper woodlands, montane at 3,500–7,500' (1,065–2,285 m); scattered among pines, dry rocky slopes, mesas

Range: throughout, except the southwestern corner

Notes: In Arizona, this widespread aster has slim leafless stalks topped by a few solitary blooms and is easily overlooked. *Filifolius* means "thread-like leaf," referring to the thin lobes of the feathery leaves that form low, round clumps of foliage (see inset). It is found in every state west of the Mississippi River. A similar species, the Mexican woollywhite (*H. mexicanus*) (not shown), is found higher in the mountains at elevations up to 10,000 feet (3,050 m).

FLOWER TYPE
Composite

LEAF TYPE
Simple

LEAF TYPE
Simple Lobed

LEAF ATTACHMENT
Alternate

LEAF ATTACHMENT
Basal

Upright Prairie Coneflower
Ratibida columnifera

Family: Aster (Asteraceae)

Height: 12–36" (30–91 cm)

Flower: cylindrical yellowish-brown cone, 1" (2.5 cm) tall, of hundreds of tiny disk flowers surrounded by 4–12 drooping oval petals (ray flowers) that are red, yellow, or bicolored; 1–15 flower heads per plant, each on a long stalk above the leaves

Leaf: stiff thin leaves, ¾–6" (2–15 cm) long, have 3–14 long, narrow, uneven lobes, are hairy and alternately attached

Bloom: Jun–Nov

Cycle/Origin: perennial; native

Zone/Habitat: all life zones except subalpine at 800–7,500' (245–2,285 m); open areas in pine forests, along roads, grassy areas, disturbed ground

Range: northeastern third of Arizona

Notes: In the wild, this drought-tolerant prairie plant is widespread in the Great Plains of the Midwest, but it is also native to Arizona. It has been used in prairie restorations. A cultivated ornamental often grown in wildflower gardens, it frequently escapes to roadsides and prairie-like habitats. The Cheyenne have used a solution from the leaves and stems to draw out poison from rattlesnake bites and for relief from poison ivy. The scientific name *columinifera* refers to the columnar shape of the flower heads

FLOWER TYPE
Composite

LEAF TYPE
Simple Lobed

LEAF ATTACHMENT
Alternate

Ghostflower
Mohavea confertiflora

Family: Plantain (Plantaginaceae)

Height: 4–16" (10–40 cm)

Flower: deeply cup-shaped, translucent yellowish or cream flowers, 1–1½" (2.5–4 cm) long, are dotted with maroon inside; fused petals form a wide upper lip and a swollen base with a large maroon spot; 2 bright-yellow male flower parts (stamens)

Leaf: lance-shaped or long and thin, fuzzy leaves, ½–4" (1–10 cm) long, with pointed tips; upper leaves stick out between flowers at top of stem

Fruit: fragile tan pod, ½" (1 cm) long, is oval and opens through top pores, spilling winged seeds

Bloom: Feb–Apr

Cycle/Origin: annual; native

Zone/Habitat: desert scrub below 3,500' (1,065 m); gravelly flats, lower mountain slopes (bajadas), along washes

Range: northwestern and southwestern corners of Arizona

Notes: This true desert annual grows a short, unbranched stem when winter rains are few and a taller, branched stem when rainfall is plentiful. It has one to many blooms (also depending on the amount of moisture the plant receives) at leaf attachments. "Ghost" is for the translucent look of its blossoms and *confertiflora* means "crowded flowers." It's found only in the lower deserts of western Arizona, southeastern California, Nevada, and into northern Mexico.

FLOWER TYPE	LEAF TYPE	LEAF ATTACHMENT	FRUIT
Irregular	**Simple**	**Alternate**	**Pod**

Plains Zinnia
Zinnia grandiflora

Family: Aster (Asteraceae)

Height: 4–12" (10–30 cm); shrub

Flower: bright-yellow flower heads, 1–1½" (2.5–4 cm) wide, have 3–6 round, shallowly notched petals (ray flowers) around a reddish-orange center (disk flowers)

Leaf: narrow leaves, 1–2" (2.5–5 cm) long, are light green, fuzzy, and twisted; densely and oppositely attached along branching stems

Bloom: May–Oct

Cycle/Origin: perennial; native

Zone/Habitat: desert scrub, grasslands, oak/pinyon pine/juniper woodlands at 4,000–6,500' (1,220–1,980 m); along roads, hillsides, mesas, among grasses, dry soils

Range: northern half and southeastern corner of Arizona

Notes: This perennial shrub forms rounded mounds of foliage nearly completely covered with long-lasting yellow flowers. The flowers persist on the plant into fall, drying and turning papery and brown. Plains zinnia spreads by underground stems (rhizomes) to form large colonies. Also called Rocky Mountain zinnia, this Aster family member ranges from Arizona east to Texas and northeast to Kansas. Often cultivated as a ground cover and used in borders, it is drought tolerant and cold hardy.

FLOWER TYPE LEAF TYPE LEAF ATTACHMENT
Composite **Simple** **Opposite**

Curlycup Gumweed
Grindelia squarrosa

Family: Aster (Asteraceae)

Height: 12–36" (30–91 cm)

Flower: yellow, daisy-like flower head, 1–1½" (2.5–4 cm) wide, sits atop layers of downward-curving green bracts; each bloom has 25–40 short, oval overlapping petals around a darker yellow center

Leaf: variable-shaped leaves, from oval to spoon-shaped, 1–3" (2.5–7.5 cm) long, have coarse-toothed edges and are dotted with glands; middle and top leaves alternately clasp the multibranched reddish stem

Bloom: Jul–Sep

Cycle/Origin: biennial, perennial; native

Zone/Habitat: grasslands, interior chaparral, woodlands of oak/pinyon pine/juniper, montane at 4,000–7,500' (1,220–2,285 m); dry open areas, overgrazed land

Range: northern half of Arizona

Notes: This aster is extremely common along roads in northern Arizona, as well as much of North America, except the southeastern states. A tea made from the leaves and flowers has been used by Plains Indigenous Peoples to treat bronchitis. The species name *squarrosa* and "curlycup" in the common name both refer to the conspicuous outward-curving bracts. The bracts have glands that exude a sticky resin, thus the name "gumweed."

FLOWER TYPE
Composite

LEAF TYPE
Simple

LEAF ATTACHMENT
Alternate

LEAF ATTACHMENT
Clasping

Threadleaf Ragwort
Senecio flaccidus

Family: Aster (Asteraceae)

Height: 1–4' (30–122 cm); shrub

Flower: daisy-like flower, 1–1½" (2.5–4 cm) wide, of non-overlapping, narrow yellow petals (usually 8–17) surrounding an orangish center of disk flowers

Leaf: thread-like, bluish-green leaves, 1½–4" (4–10 cm) long, divided into very narrow lobes, smooth or woolly and covered with matted gray hairs; leaves are alternately attached to the stiff stem

Bloom: May–Nov, but year-round in low elevations

Cycle/Origin: perennial; native

Zone/Habitat: desert scrub, grasslands, and interior chaparral at 2,500–7,500' (760–2,285 m); along sandy washes, disturbed or overgrazed lands, flats, plateaus

Range: throughout

Notes: This many-stemmed, multibranched, bluish-green shrub has bright-yellow flowers on long stalks at the end of the branches. Abundant in disturbed soils or overgrazed lands, it stabilizes the soil, which helps other plants to become established. It's toxic if eaten by livestock, but Indigenous Peoples have used this plant medicinally. The Navajo have boiled the plant to aid their voices in ceremonial singing and used the flower heads to brush spines off of cactus fruit.

FLOWER TYPE
Composite

LEAF TYPE
Simple Lobed

LEAF ATTACHMENT
Alternate

Angelita Daisy
Tetraneuris acaulis

Family: Aster (Asteraceae)

Height: 3–12" (7.5–30 cm)

Flower: daisy-like flower head, 1–2" (2.5–5 cm) wide, has 8–15 long, narrow, non-overlapping yellow petals that have dark lines on the undersides, 3-lobed tips, and surround a yellow center

Leaf: narrowly lance-shaped basal leaves, ¾–2½" (2–6 cm) long, with pointed tips and densely dotted with glands that make them sticky

Bloom: Apr–Oct

Cycle/Origin: perennial; native

Zone/Habitat: pinyon pine/juniper woodlands and montane at 4,000–6,000' (1,220–1,830 m); among ponderosa pines, plateaus, rocky slopes

Range: northern half of Arizona, often planted in gardens in Phoenix

Notes: Also known as Arizona four-nerve daisy, this cheery yellow flower is often grown in gardens at low elevations. It is especially popular among Phoenix gardeners because it is drought tolerant and hardy in temperatures as low as 10°F (-12°C). Even in desert locations, this plant blooms most of the summer if watered weekly. The yellow blooms top leafless, slightly fuzzy flower stalks well above the basal rosette of leaves, but this plant has no leafy stems. In fact, the species name acaulis is Greek, meaning "without stems."

FLOWER TYPE   LEAF TYPE   LEAF ATTACHMENT
Composite   **Simple**   **Basal**

Arizona Yellowbells

Tecoma stans

Family: Trumpet Creeper (Bignoniaceae)

Height: 2–15' (0.6–4.6 m); shrub

Flower: groups of 2–7 trumpet-shaped golden flowers, 1–2" (2.5–5 cm) long, with orange-striped throats; each flower has 5 fused petals that flare into rounded notched lobes and a short crown-like green calyx

Leaf: shiny, dark-green leaves, 6" (15 cm) long, divided into 5–13 narrowly oval leaflets, 2–5" (5–13 cm) long, with pointed tips and sharp-toothed edges

Fruit: long, thin, dangling tan pod, 3–8" (7.5–20 cm) long

Bloom: May–Oct

Cycle/Origin: perennial; native

Zone/Habitat: desert scrub, grasslands, oak/juniper woodlands at 3,000–5,500' (915–1,675 m); rocky slopes, canyons

Range: southeastern quarter of Arizona, often cultivated throughout the state

Notes: Found in only four states in the wild in the US, it occurs naturally and abundantly along Box Canyon Road in the Santa Rita Mountains, located south of Tucson. This stunning bush is evergreen in frost-free areas, attaining woody stems and its maximum, tree-like height. When frozen back to the ground in temperatures near 20°F (-7°C), it recovers readily and sends out new green shoots the next spring, but it doesn't grow more than 3 feet (0.9 m) tall.

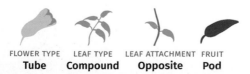

FLOWER TYPE **Tube** LEAF TYPE **Compound** LEAF ATTACHMENT **Opposite** FRUIT **Pod**

New Mexico Groundsel
Packera neomexicana

Family: Aster (Asteraceae)

Height: 8–20" (20–50 cm)

Flower: yellow, relatively flat cluster, 1–2" (2.5–5 cm) wide, of 3–20 composite flower heads, each 1" (2.5 cm) wide, made up of 5–8 (sometimes 13) petals surrounding a darker-yellow center; cluster is shaped like an open umbrella

Leaf: basal leaves, oval to narrowly lance-shaped, ¾–2½" (2–6 cm) long, with woolly hairs, variable margins; the few stem leaves are smaller going up the stem

Bloom: Apr–Aug

Cycle/Origin: perennial; native

Zone/Habitat: interior chaparral, montane and subalpine at 3,000–9,000' (915–2,745 m); dry hillsides, meadows

Range: throughout, except the southwestern corner

Notes: It's the most common of 10 species of *Packera* in Arizona. These species are often called DYCs for "darn yellow composites," since they are so difficult to distinguish from each other as the result of hybridization. It's also called New Mexico butterweed for the buttery color of the flowers, which are loosely grouped or in dense clusters at the top of the branching flower stalk. The tall, almost leafless flower stalk is typical of this plant. The basal rosette's density and number of leaves depend on the amount of rainfall where the plant grows.

CLUSTER TYPE **Flat**   FLOWER TYPE **Composite**   LEAF TYPE **Simple**   LEAF TYPE **Simple Lobed**   LEAF ATTACHMENT **Alternate**   LEAF ATTACHMENT **Basal**

Hartweg Sundrops
Calylophus hartwegii

Family: Evening-primrose (Onagraceae)

Height: 12–16" (30–40 cm)

Flower: large yellow (fading to pinkish) flower, 1–2½" (2.5–6 cm) wide, made up of 4 wide (almost square) wrinkled petals; center is same color as the petals

Leaf: narrowly oval, grayish-green basal leaves, ½–1½" (1–4 cm) long, have fuzzy stem leaves; sometimes clusters of smaller leaves grow in leaf attachments

Fruit: 4-parted, cylindrical green pod, ¼–1½" (0.6–4 cm) long, fuzzy with white hairs, has many tiny seeds

Bloom: Apr–Jun

Cycle/Origin: perennial; native

Zone/Habitat: grasslands and pinyon pine/juniper woodlands at 3,000–7,000' (915–2,135 m); hillsides, plains

Range: northeastern and southeastern corners of Arizona, covering two-thirds of the state

Notes: Hardy and drought tolerant, Hartweg sundrops is often cultivated in rock gardens as ground cover. The masses of blooms on this low-growing evergreen plant attract hawk moths. Flowers open in the afternoon or near sunset and bloom until the next afternoon, when they are replaced by more buds. Indigenous Peoples have used this plant to treat internal bleeding. Though found only as far west as Arizona, it ranges eastward to Texas and northward to Kansas.

FLOWER TYPE	LEAF TYPE	LEAF ATTACHMENT	LEAF ATTACHMENT	FRUIT
Regular	**Simple**	**Alternate**	**Basal**	**Pod**

Summer Poppy
Kallstroemia grandiflora

Family: Caltrop (Zygophyllaceae)

Height: 1–4' (30–122 cm)

Flower: round and flat or bowl-shaped, orangish-yellow flowers, 1–2½" (2.5–6 cm) wide, with dark-reddish-orange centers, made up of 5 broad fan-shaped petals with dark-reddish-orange lines and bases; blossoms top long hairy stalks

Leaf: feather-like, dark-green leaves, 1–3" (2.5–7.5 cm) long, are divided into 4–8 pairs of elliptical leaflets, opposite on hairy sprawling or erect stems

Bloom: Jul–Oct, after monsoon rains begin

Cycle/Origin: annual; native

Zone/Habitat: desert scrub and grasslands at 1,000–5,000' (305–1,525 m); along roads and sandy washes, flats, slopes, mesas, disturbed areas

Range: southernmost quarter of Arizona and the west-central part of the state

Notes: This sprawling annual has orangish-yellow flowers on erect hairy stems. Its blooms are sometimes mistaken for the four-petaled flowers of the spring-blooming California poppy (pg. 363), which is not related. After heavy summer monsoons, this showy flower covers large patches of grasslands and roadsides. Although found in southern California, summer poppy is not native there and is common only in southern Arizona, western Texas, and northern Mexico.

FLOWER TYPE
Regular

LEAF TYPE
Compound

LEAF ATTACHMENT
Opposite

Mountain Parsley

Pseudocymopterus montanus

Family: Carrot (Apiaceae)

Height: 10–24" (25–61 cm)

Flower: small clusters (umbels) of tiny flowers forming larger, golden-yellow or orangish-red flat clusters, 1–3" (2.5–7.5 cm) wide

Leaf: extremely variable leaves (can be lobed, compound, or twice compound), 2–6" (5–15 cm) long, are finely divided into leaflets of various sizes and shapes

Fruit: oblong ridged green capsule, ¼" (0.6 cm) long, turns bright red when mature

Bloom: May–Oct

Cycle/Origin: perennial; native

Zone/Habitat: grasslands, montane, subalpine at 5,500–11,500' (1,675–3,510 m); meadows, aspen groves

Range: northern half and southeastern corner of Arizona

Notes: The height, leaves, and flowers of mountain parsley are highly variable. The odorous leaves are sometimes feather-like and differ in how many times they are divided. The leaflets vary greatly in size and shape, from wide and lobed to narrow with smooth edges. Interestingly, the flowers can vary from golden yellow to orangish red on the same plant. It's a member of the Carrot family, which includes plants with hollow stems such as common garden parsley, carrot, and dill. It's also called alpine false spring parsley.

CLUSTER TYPE	FLOWER TYPE	LEAF TYPE	LEAF TYPE	LEAF ATTACHMENT	FRUIT
Flat	**Regular**	**Simple Lobed**	**Twice Compound**	**Basal**	**Pod**

white form

California Poppy
Eschscholzia californica

Family: Poppy (Papaveraceae)

Height: 2–16" (5–40 cm)

Flower: shallowly cup-shaped, yellow or orangish-yellow flower, 1½" (4 cm) wide, has 4 fan-shaped petals, each with an orange spot at the base; each flower on a single stalk; many flowers per plant

Leaf: fern-like, bluish-green basal leaves, 2½" (6 cm) long, with 3 thin rounded lobes; few stem leaves

Fruit: erect, cylindrical, pointed green pod, 4" (10 cm) long, splits open to release tiny black seeds

Bloom: middle Feb–May

Cycle/Origin: annual; native

Zone/Habitat: desert scrub below 4,600' (1,400 m); flats, slopes

Range: throughout, except the northeastern part of the state

Notes: The blooms of California poppy remain open only in full sunlight, closing at night and when cloudy. After heavy winter rains, acres of desert floor are densely carpeted with the gold flowers of California poppy mixed with arroyo lupine (pg. 43) and fiddleneck (pg. 419). Blooms can be pinkish white or white (see inset). Sometimes hikers find the flowers on stalks that are thigh-high. The small annual poppies in Arizona were long considered to be a separate species called Mexican poppy (*E. mexicana*), but they are now thought to be a subspecies of California poppy.

FLOWER TYPE
Regular

LEAF TYPE
Simple Lobed

LEAF ATTACHMENT
Alternate

LEAF ATTACHMENT
Basal

FRUIT
Pod

seed head

Pale Agoseris
Agoseris glauca

Family: Aster (Asteraceae)

Height: 1–10" (2.5–25 cm)

Flower: dandelion-like yellow flower head, 1½" (4 cm) wide, has layers of numerous yellow petals (ray flowers) with dark lines below and notched tips, around a few yellow flower parts; held by a hairy, triangular purple-spotted green bract; flower tops a single leafless hairy stem

Leaf: narrow, grass-like or lance-shaped basal leaves, 6–14" (15–36 cm) long, are purplish blue-green or with a purplish central vein

Bloom: May–Oct

Cycle/Origin: perennial; native

Zone/Habitat: higher desert scrub, montane, subalpine at 6,500–10,000' (1,980–3,050 m); among coniferous trees, along roads, in sagebrush scrub

Range: northern half of Arizona, scattered in the south-central part of the state

Notes: It's also called mountain dandelion for the flower heads and resulting fluffy globe-like seed heads (see inset), which look very much like the smaller puffballs of common dandelion (pg. 420). The hairy leafless stems contain a milky sap. It was collected by Lewis and Clark on their famous expedition to the American West. *Glauca* means "blue-green" in Latin, referring to the color of the leaves.

FLOWER TYPE
Composite

LEAF TYPE
Simple

LEAF ATTACHMENT
Basal

365

Heartleaf Buttercup

Ranunculus cardiophyllus

Family: Buttercup (Ranunculaceae)

Height: 6–21" (15–53 cm)

Flower: groups of 1–5 round butter-yellow flowers, each flower 1½" (3.8 cm) wide, with 5 round waxy petals around a green center of many flower parts

Leaf: moist-appearing, bright-green leaves, ¾–2⅓" (2–6 cm) long, are variable; basal leaves are usually heart-shaped on long stems with finely scalloped edges; stem leaves are elliptical and deeply lobed, alternate on erect stems

Bloom: June–July

Cycle/Origin: perennial; native

Zone/Habitat: montane and subalpine, in moist areas and dry mountain meadows at 7,000–11,155' (2,134–3,400 m) near pine, spruce, or fir trees

Range: northeastern third of state

Notes: One to five bright-yellow flowers top the erect stems and branches of this mountain plant that occurs in high meadows ranging from Arizona north through southwestern Canada. There are 19 species of buttercups in Arizona, and heartleaf is named for the shape of its leaves. Buttercups contain a poison that affects the heart if eaten by livestock or people. The flowers produce little nectar but much nutritious pollen, thereby attracting pollen-eating beetles, flies, and bees.

FLOWER TYPE
Regular

LEAF TYPE
Simple

LEAF TYPE
Simple Lobed

LEAF ATTACHMENT
Alternate

LEAF ATTACHMENT
Basal

367

Golden Crownbeard
Verbesina encelioides

Family: Aster (Asteraceae)

Height: 4–20" (10–50 cm)

Flower: layers of 12–15 (or many more) overlapping rectangular petals (ray flowers) with 3-lobed tips surround the wide orange center of this daisy-like yellow flower head, 1½–2" (4–5 cm) wide; each flower is backed by many pointed grayish bracts

Leaf: broadly triangular leaves, ½–6" (3–15 cm) long, are grayish green and have irregular-toothed margins; lower leaves mostly alternate, upper leaves opposite; opposite pairs of smaller, leaf-like appendages (stipules) at base of each leafstalk

Bloom: Mar–Dec

Cycle/Origin: annual; native

Zone/Habitat: desert scrub, grasslands, oak/pinyon pine/juniper woodlands below 6,000' (1,830 m); along washes

Range: throughout

Notes: It's a common annual abundant along roads and in disturbed soils, especially where extra water is found, such as in the floodplains near washes. Eye-catching, bright-yellow, daisy-like blooms top this erect plant. "Crownbeard" is for the seed-like fruit topped with gray-brown hairs. Ants, birds, and rodents eat the seeds. Indigenous Peoples have used infusions of plant parts to treat skin diseases and spider bites and have consumed it as a tea to treat stomach disorders.

FLOWER TYPE **Composite**   LEAF TYPE **Simple**   LEAF ATTACHMENT **Alternate**   LEAF ATTACHMENT **Opposite**

Brittlebush

Encelia farinosa

Family: Aster (Asteraceae)

Height: 1–5' (30–152 cm); shrub

Flower: daisy-like yellow flower head, 1½–2" (4–5 cm) wide, made up of 11–21 lobed petals (ray flowers) around a yellow-to-purplish-brown center; groups of flower heads top stalks well above the leaves

Leaf: oval or lance-shaped, bluish-green leaves, ¾–3½" (2–9 cm) long, are hairy above with pointed or rounded tips; leaves are clustered near tips of multibranched whitish stems; stems are covered with matted hairs until older, turning smooth barked

Bloom: Nov–May

Cycle/Origin: perennial; native

Zone/Habitat: desert scrub, grasslands below 3,500' (1,065 m); flats, rocky slopes, along washes

Range: throughout Arizona, except the northeastern and southeastern parts of the state

Notes: Named for its brittle stems, this is usually a mounded bush in full sun, but it can become leggy when shaded or overwatered. The flower heads are borne on thin flower stalks above the grayish-green foliage. It's drought deciduous, with the leaves turning brown and dropping off during drought; new leaves sprout when it rains. The sap in the stems was burned as incense by early missionaries, thus another common name, incienso (Spanish for "incense").

FLOWER TYPE
Composite

LEAF TYPE
Simple

LEAF ATTACHMENT
Opposite

371

Adonis Blazing Star
Mentzelia multiflora

Family: Loasa (Loasaceae)

Height: 6–36" (15–91 cm)

Flower: star-shaped yellow flower, 1½–3" (4–7.5 cm) wide, streaked with orange, has 10 narrow-to-broad, pointed petals around many long flower parts, with the outer flattened flower parts resembling petals

Leaf: lance-shaped basal leaves, ½–2" (1–15 cm) long, are bluish green, have hook-shaped hairs, variable margins; upper stem leaves much smaller than lower

Fruit: hairy, greenish-tan capsule, ⅓–⅔" (0.8–1.6 cm) long, cylindrical, cup-shaped at top, tapered base, wick-like center, and twisted persistent sepals on edges

Bloom: Apr–Jun

Cycle/Origin: perennial, biennial; native

Zone/Habitat: desert scrub at 100–2,500' (30–760 m); roadsides, along washes, among creosote bushes

Range: throughout

Notes: Adonis blazing star flowers open in the late afternoon. It's one of 23 species of *Mentzelia* in Arizona, most with unusually intricate flowers. The seedpods are as complex as the flowers; each seedpod resembles a candle with a wick in the center, but the top rim is ringed with persistent spider-like sepals. It ranges from southern California to western Texas to southern Wyoming.

FLOWER TYPE
Regular

LEAF TYPE
Simple

LEAF TYPE
Simple Lobed

LEAF ATTACHMENT
Alternate

FRUIT
Pod

Western Wallflower
Erysimum capitatum

Family: Mustard (Brassicaceae)

Height: 12–32" (30–80 cm)

Flower: many small yellow-to-orange flowers, ¾" (2 cm) wide, in a nearly round or cylindrical cluster, 1½–3½" (4–11 cm) wide; each flower has 4 oval petals, protruding green flower parts, and long green sepals (calyx); cluster blooms from the bottom up

Leaf: basal rosette of narrowly lance-shaped leaves; 1–5" (2.5–13 cm) long, have pointed tips and are on short stalks; erect stem leaves are stalkless

Fruit: erect pod-like green container, turning brown, 2–4" (5–10 cm) long, has 4 sides; is long, thin, and fleshy

Bloom: Mar–Sep

Cycle/Origin: perennial, biennial; native

Zone/Habitat: all life zones above 2,500' (760 m); slopes, canyons

Range: throughout, except the southwestern corner

Notes: The name "wallflower" comes from a close relative from Eurasia that is often found growing on stone walls. The species name *capitatum* is Latin for "head" and refers to the head-shaped cluster of flowers. In coniferous forests above 7,000 feet (2,135 m), the flowers of this very common native mustard are orange. This orange variety was once considered a separate species, but it is now thought that western wallflower is just an extremely variable plant.

CLUSTER TYPE	FLOWER TYPE	LEAF TYPE	LEAF ATTACHMENT	LEAF ATTACHMENT	FRUIT
Round	**Regular**	**Simple**	**Alternate**	**Basal**	**Pod**

Smooth Desert Dandelion
Malacothrix glabrata

Family: Aster (Asteraceae)

Height: 4–16" (10–40 cm)

Flower: yellow-and-white flower heads, 2" (5 cm) wide, on long stalks; each bloom has no disk flowers, only long narrow petals (ray flowers) tipped with 5 tiny teeth, center is red until all the ray flowers open, then turns dark yellow; outer rims of petals are white

Leaf: basal, dark-green, feathery leaves, 2–6" (5–15 cm) long, deeply divided into 3–6 pairs of thread-like lobes with pointed tips

Bloom: Mar–Jun

Cycle/Origin: annual; native

Zone/Habitat: desert scrub below 6,000' (1,830 m); mesas, among creosote bushes and saltbushes, under Joshua trees

Range: western two-thirds of Arizona

Notes: Widespread across the West from Montana to Texas, this low-growing, multibranching annual grows in sandy or gravelly soils. *Malacothrix* means "soft hair" and refers to the usual fuzziness of young plants in this genus, but this species is called *glabrata* for its smoothness and lack of hairs. After heavy winter rains, this wildflower carpets large areas of desert with blooming plants growing in circles similar to fairy rings (mushrooms sprouting around decaying underground material), benefiting baby desert tortoises, which feed on the foliage.

FLOWER TYPE
Composite

LEAF TYPE
Simple Lobed

LEAF ATTACHMENT
Alternate

LEAF ATTACHMENT
Basal

377

Red Dome Blanketflower
Gaillardia pinnatifida

Family: Aster (Asteraceae)

Height: 6–16" (15–40 cm)

Flower: yellow flower head, 2" (5 cm) wide, has 5–14 short or long petals (ray flowers) with 3-lobed tips around a fuzzy, domed, dark-reddish center (disk flowers)

Leaf: finely hairy basal leaves, 1–2½" (2.5–6 cm) long, are grayish green and lance-shaped to thin; some leaves on each plant have rounded lobes

Bloom: May–Oct

Cycle/Origin: perennial; native

Zone/Habitat: desert scrub, grasslands, oak/pinyon pine/juniper woods, montane at 3,500–7,000' (1,065–2,135 m); plains, mesas, clearings among ponderosa pines

Range: throughout, except the southwestern quarter

Notes: It's found from Nevada southeast to Texas and Oklahoma, often along roads. It's frequently included in western wildflower seed mixtures, as it grows readily from seed. The basal clump of leaves sends up long slim flower stalks, so the blooms bounce and sway in the wind. The variety found in Arizona has more undivided and narrower leaves than the wider, many-lobed leaves of plants occurring in other states. The genus *Gaillardia* was named after M. Gaillard de Charentonneau, a French magistrate who supported the studies of botanists in the 18th century.

FLOWER TYPE	LEAF TYPE	LEAF TYPE	LEAF ATTACHMENT	LEAF ATTACHMENT
Composite	**Simple**	**Simple Lobed**	**Alternate**	**Basal**

Desert Marigold
Baileya multiradiata

Family: Aster (Asteraceae)

Height: 8–36" (20–91 cm)

Flower: daisy-like, lemon-yellow flower head, 2" (5 cm) wide, of multiple layers of 34–55 overlapping petals with tooth-like edges surrounding as many as 100 tiny disk flowers; flower head on long flower stalk

Leaf: rosette of oval, grayish-green basal leaves, 1¼–4" (3–10 cm) long, are fuzzy with edges smooth or lobed and resembling the barbs of a feather; stem leaves are much fewer and smaller in the summer

Bloom: Mar-Oct, after rainfall

Cycle/Origin: annual, perennial, biennial; native

Zone/Habitat: desert scrub at 500–5,000' (152–1,525 m); on flats, slopes, along roads, mesas

Range: throughout, except the northwestern corner

Notes: Found only in the Southwest, this is one of the longest-blooming and most common wildflowers in Arizona, often covering hillsides with a yellow haze in spring. Poisonous to sheep and goats, it contains chemicals proven to have anticancer properties. It's easily grown from seed, but it's intolerant of temperatures below 32°F (0°C). In autumn, when desert marigold grows smaller flower heads with fewer ray flowers, it is easily confused with woolly desert marigold (*B. pleniradiata*) (not shown), which always has smaller flower heads and fewer ray flowers.

FLOWER TYPE
Composite

LEAF TYPE
Simple Lobed

LEAF ATTACHMENT
Alternate

LEAF ATTACHMENT
Basal

Desert Evening-primrose
Oenothera primiveris

Family: Evening-primrose (Onagraceae)

Height: 4–6" (10–15 cm)

Flower: yellow flower, 2" (5 cm) wide, turns reddish orange when wilted, has 4 broadly heart-shaped petals and 4 hairy, horn-shaped, downward-curving sepals

Leaf: dandelion-like, blunted, lance-shaped green leaves, 1½–11" (4–28 cm) long, coarse-haired, deep irregular lobes; leaves flat or partially erect in basal rosette

Fruit: cylindrical greenish capsules, ½–2½" (1–6 cm) long, sticky red spots, white hairs, 4-winged, open at top

Bloom: middle Feb–May

Cycle/Origin: perennial; native

Zone/Habitat: desert scrub, oak/pinyon pine/juniper woods below 5,300' (1,615 m); sandy flats, rocky slopes, arroyos

Range: northwestern and southern Arizona, ranging over two-thirds of the state

Notes: This low, stemless plant has fragrant, pale-yellow flowers that are remarkably large compared to its rosette of dandelion-like leaves. Found throughout the Southwest, from southern California to western Texas, it's common in the Cabeza Prieta National Wildlife Refuge in southwestern Arizona. Like other evening-primroses, this wildflower opens in the evening; unlike other species, it stays open much of the next day.

FLOWER TYPE
Regular

LEAF TYPE
Simple Lobed

LEAF ATTACHMENT
Basal

FRUIT
Pod

Desert Rose Mallow
Hibiscus coulteri

Family: Mallow (Malvaceae)

Height: 1–4' (30–122 cm); shrub

Flower: bowl-shaped flowers of pale yellow to creamy white, 2" (5 cm) wide, have 5 overlapping broad petals with red-streaked bases around a yellow-and-maroon center; each bloom cupped by 14 thread-like pointed green bracts

Leaf: lower oval and undivided leaves, 1½" (4 cm) long; upper hairy leaves, 1" (2.5 cm) long, have 3 narrow lobes with toothed reddish edges; leaves drop in winter

Fruit: star-shaped tan capsule contains seeds covered with long hairs

Bloom: Feb–Nov, after rain

Cycle/Origin: perennial; native

Zone/Habitat: desert scrub at 1,500–4,500' (460–1,370 m); canyon walls, rocky slopes, limestone soils

Range: southern half of Arizona

Notes: This straggling, sparsely branched shrub is leafy above and woody below. The spindly stems are weak, so it usually grows up through other shrubs for support. The lowest flowers on the stems open first. In the wild, it's found only in southern Arizona, southern New Mexico, western Texas, and northern Mexico. Often cultivated, it requires little water to keep it blooming most of the year.

FLOWER TYPE
Regular

LEAF TYPE
Simple

LEAF TYPE
Simple Lobed

LEAF ATTACHMENT
Alternate

FRUIT
Pod

Desert Unicorn Plant
Proboscidea altheifolia

Family: Martynia (Martyniaceae)

Height: 1–2½' (30–76 cm); vine

Flower: yellow tubular flower, 2" (5 cm) long, has orange dotted lines in throat; mouth of tube has 2 lips; upper split and wavy lip bends backward, lower broad-bulging lip is horizontal; flowers in groups above the leaves

Leaf: rounded heart-shaped leaves, 1–3" (2.5–7.5 cm) wide, shiny, wrinkled with 3–5 lobes or scalloped edges; long stalks; hairy sticky sprawling stems

Fruit: fuzzy, curved, tapered brown pod, 6" (15 cm) long, opens lengthwise into 2 curving sharp "claws"

Bloom: Jul–Sep

Cycle/Origin: perennial; native

Zone/Habitat: desert scrub below 4,000' (1,220 m); sandy flats, among creosote bushes

Range: southern half of Arizona and the northwestern corner of the state

Notes: This perennial is closely related to the annual devil's claw (pg. 243), but it has yellow blooms above its shiny leaves instead of white-and-purple flowers hidden below fuzzy leaves. Both have curved, dry claw-like seedpods that attach to the legs of passing animals, dispersing seeds. Desert unicorn plant has a thick root that sprouts foliage or flowers only after the monsoons begin.

FLOWER TYPE
Tube

LEAF TYPE
Simple Lobed

LEAF ATTACHMENT
Opposite

FRUIT
Pod

387

Showy Goldeneye
Heliomeris multiflora

Family: Aster (Asteraceae)

Height: 12–36" (30–91 cm)

Flower: yellow flower head, 2½" (6 cm) wide, has 8–15 yellow petals (ray flowers) around a darker-yellow flat center (disk flowers) that becomes cone-shaped as petals wilt; each bloom held by green bracts

Leaf: long, narrow, stiffly hairy leaves, ¾–2½" (2–6 cm) long, are oppositely attached to branching stems

Bloom: Jul–Oct

Cycle/Origin: perennial; native

Zone/Habitat: grasslands, oak/pinyon pine/juniper woodlands and montane at 4,500–9,000' (1,370–2,745 m); among ponderosa pines, roadsides, meadows, rocky slopes, upland valleys, disturbed soils

Range: throughout most of Arizona, except in the southwestern corner

Notes: Showy goldeneye is widespread in the West, especially wherever disturbed soils occur, such as where prairie dogs or gophers dig holes or mounds. Often planted along roads by the state highway department, this showy sunflower is common on the North and South Rims of the Grand Canyon from July through October. The Navajo have used the seeds for food and the plant for sheep fodder.

FLOWER TYPE
Composite

LEAF TYPE
Simple

LEAF ATTACHMENT
Opposite

Hairy Desert Sunflower

Geraea canescens

Family: Aster (Asteraceae)

Height: 4–32" (10–80 cm)

Flower: typical yellow sunflower head, 2–3" (5–7.5 cm) wide, has 10–21 oblong 3-lobed petals around a golden-orange center; flower heads single or in groups topping the stems well above the leaves

Leaf: hairy, grayish-green leaves, ½–4" (1–10 cm) long, are oval or lance-shaped with smooth or toothed edges and pointed tips; lower leaves more numerous and on winged leafstalks; upper leaves stalkless

Bloom: Oct–Jun, but especially common in April

Cycle/Origin: annual; native

Zone/Habitat: desert scrub below 4,500' (1,370 m); along washes

Range: western half of Arizona

Notes: The genus name *Geraea*, from the Greek word for "old," refers to the white-haired leaves, stems, bracts, and seeds. Rodents and birds eat the seeds, but enough remain in the soil to produce new plants the following year. This showy sunflower is extremely abundant after heavy rains, and along with desert sand verbena (pg. 167) and dune evening-primrose (pg. 267), miles of roadsides and sandy desert flats or valleys are covered with a spectacular display of blooms. Sadly, many desert areas where these beautiful wildflowers once grew are being overrun by the invasive exotic Sahara mustard (*Brassica tournefortii*) (not shown).

FLOWER TYPE LEAF TYPE LEAF ATTACHMENT
Composite **Simple** **Alternate**

Transpecos Thimblehead
Hymenothrix wislizeni

Family: Aster (Asteraceae)

Height: 12–28" (30–71 cm)

Flower: flat-topped, branched, orangish-yellow cluster, 2–6" (5–15 cm) wide, of many small flower heads; each flower head has 3–8 narrow toothed yellow petals (ray flowers) around a yellow center of 15–30 disk flowers; several clusters per plant

Leaf: leaves are divided into 3 narrow, irregular shaped lobes; each leaf, 1–5" (2.5–13 cm) long, is alternately attached to a branched stem; most of the leaves are near the base; the upper leaves are much smaller

Bloom: Jun–Dec

Cycle/Origin: annual, biennial; native

Zone/Habitat: desert scrub and grasslands at 2,000–5,000' (600–1,500 m); along roads and washes, slopes

Range: southern half of Arizona, except the southwestern edge of the state

Notes: "Transpecos" is the region in western Texas, near the Pecos River, where this plant was first found. "Thimblehead" is for the resemblance of its unopened flower head buds to a sewing thimble. This common roadside weed is also called Wislizenus beeflower for the powerful attraction of its flowers to bees. There are more than 1,000 different species of wild bees found near Tucson. The foliage of this wildflower is eaten by javelinas (pig-like animals).

CLUSTER TYPE	FLOWER TYPE	LEAF TYPE	LEAF ATTACHMENT
Flat	**Composite**	**Simple Lobed**	**Alternate**

Yellow Owl's Clover
Orthocarpus luteus

Family: Broomrape (Orobanchaceae)

Height: 4–16" (10–40 cm)

Flower: spike clusters, 2–8" (5–20 cm) long, of 2-lipped yellow flowers, ½" (1 cm) long; flowers are partially hidden by conspicuous, 3-lobed, purplish-green bracts covered with sticky, glistening white hairs

Leaf: narrow dark-green leaves, ½–2" (1–5 cm) long, have smooth edges; upper leaves have 3 lobes; alternately attached, spiraling up the stem

Fruit: straight-sided tan pods, ¼" (0.6 cm) long

Bloom: Jul–Sep

Cycle/Origin: annual; native

Zone/Habitat: higher oak/pinyon pine/juniper woodlands, montane, subalpine at 7,000–9,500' (2,135–2,895 m); among coniferous trees, moist meadows, in sagebrush scrub, slopes

Range: northern half of Arizona

Notes: *Orthocarpus* means "straight fruit" in Greek, referring to the seedpods. Famous botanist Thomas Nuttall collected this annual in North Dakota in the early 1800s and named the genus. The small roots of this semiparasitic plant invade the roots of other plants to obtain part of their nutrition. This slender leafy plant is the most widespread of owl's clover, ranging to California, Washington, western Minnesota, and New Mexico.

CLUSTER TYPE	FLOWER TYPE	LEAF TYPE	LEAF TYPE	LEAF ATTACHMENT	FRUIT
Spike	**Irregular**	**Simple**	**Simple Lobed**	**Alternate**	**Pod**

Turpentinebush
Ericameria laricifolia

Family: Aster (Asteraceae)

Height: 12–36" (30–91 cm); shrub

Flower: daisy-like yellow flower heads, each ⅜" (0.9 cm) wide, with 3–6 petals and a ragged yellow-orange center; flowers form a dense flat cluster, 3" (7.5 cm) wide; highest cluster on the plant blooms first

Leaf: needle-like, leathery, grayish-green leaves, ½–1½" (1–4 cm) long, are erect and sticky; erect, nearly parallel branches grow closely together

Bloom: Aug–Dec

Cycle/Origin: perennial; native

Zone/Habitat: desert scrub, pinyon pine/juniper woods at 3,000–6,000' (915–1,830 m); canyons, creosote bush flats, mountain slopes, rocky cliffs, mesas

Range: southern half and northwestern quarter of Arizona

Notes: The stems and leaves, when crushed, exude a resin that smells like turpentine, thus part of the plant's common name. Turpentinebush is a showy bloomer covering hillsides with yellow masses in the fall. It retains the fluffy, dandelion-like, tan flower parts through the winter. This low-growing evergreen shrub forms a compact mound that needs no trimming and is attractive in desert landscaping, even when not in bloom. Cultivated varieties can be seen on highway medians. It tolerates heat and cold down to 32° F (0°C), while requiring little water once established.

CLUSTER TYPE	FLOWER TYPE	LEAF TYPE	LEAF ATTACHMENT
Flat	**Composite**	**Simple**	**Alternate**

Nodding Sunflower
Helianthella quinquenervis

Family: Aster (Asteraceae)

Height: 2–5' (61–152 cm)

Flower: composite yellow sunflower, 3" (7.5 cm) wide, has 13–21 slender petals (ray flowers) surrounding a greenish-yellow center and is held by sticky fuzzy bracts; drooping flower head found singly or in small groups atop the gray-haired stems

Leaf: wide lance-shaped basal leaves, 4–20" (10–50 cm) long, are grayish green, hairy, and have 5 prominent veins; a few opposite stem leaves

Bloom: Jul–Oct

Cycle/Origin: perennial; native

Zone/Habitat: grasslands, montane, subalpine at 5,000–10,000' (1,525–3,050 m); moist meadows, aspen grove and coniferous forest clearings, banks of streams

Range: eastern third of Arizona

Notes: *Helianthella* is Greek for "little sunflower" and *quinquenervis* is Latin for "five-nerved," referring to the veins in the leaves. When ripe, the whole sunflower seed heads are eaten by elk, deer, and bears. Compounds in the roots are being investigated for their ability to fight fungal infections. Nectar containing lots of sugar and amino acids is secreted from the bracts of the flower heads and is consumed by ants. The ants, in return, defend the flower against egg-laying flies, whose larvae would eat the developing seeds.

FLOWER TYPE
Composite

LEAF TYPE
Simple

LEAF ATTACHMENT
Opposite

LEAF ATTACHMENT
Basal

Golden Columbine

Aquilegia chrysantha

Family: Buttercup (Ranunculaceae)

Height: 1–4' (30–122 cm)

Flower: large, drooping, bright-yellow flower, 3" (7.5 cm) wide, 5 petals and 5 backward-curving, paler-yellow sepals; each petal has a nectar-filled spur

Leaf: fern-like, bluish-green basal leaves, 3½–18" (9–45 cm) long, divided 2 (can be 3) times into leaflets; each lobed leaflet, 1½" (4 cm) long, is the shape of a piece of pie; stem leaves fewer and smaller

Fruit: green pod, turning brown and papery with age, 1¼–2" (3–5 cm) long, splits along its side to release many shiny round seeds

Bloom: Apr–Sep

Cycle/Origin: perennial; native

Zone/Habitat: riparian deciduous, montane, subalpine at 3,000–11,000' (915–3,355 m); in pine forests, mountains, canyons, seeps, along streams, rich moist soils

Range: throughout, except the southwestern corner

Notes: The genus name *Aquilegia* is from the Latin *aquila*, meaning "eagle" and refers to the five curving spurs that resemble the talons of an eagle. The species name *chrysantha* means "golden flowered." The showy fragrant flowers attract hummingbirds, butterflies, hawk moths, and bumblebees to its nectar-filled spurs. It's the most common and widespread of the seven wild columbines in Arizona.

FLOWER TYPE
Irregular

LEAF TYPE
Twice Compound

LEAF ATTACHMENT
Alternate

LEAF ATTACHMENT
Basal

FRUIT
Pod

Hooker Evening-primrose
Oenothera elata

Family: Evening-primrose (Onagraceae)

Height: 2–8' (.6–2.4 m)

Flower: lemon-yellow flower (fading to reddish orange), 3" (7.5 cm) wide, has 4 broad heart-shaped petals and 4 narrow downward-curving sepals

Leaf: leaves lance-shaped to elliptical, 1½–10" (4–25 cm) long, with toothed margins and pointed tips; red stem has sticky hairs with blister-like red bases

Fruit: narrow tapering green pod, ¾–3" (2–7.5 cm) long, turns tan, contains pitted seeds

Bloom: Jul–Oct

Cycle/Origin: biennial, native

Zone/Habitat: pinyon pine/juniper woodlands and montane at 4,000–9,500' (1,220–2,895 m); wet ditches, along roads, clearings among ponderosa pines, moist soils

Range: throughout, except the southwestern corner

Notes: The species name *elata*, which is Latin for "tall," describes this plant well. Found at medium-to-high elevations, this statuesque plant of coniferous forests has large, bright-yellow flowers and bright-green leaves growing all along its six (or more) red stems. It forms a basal rosette the first year, sending up the long leafy stalk and blooming during the second. Flowers open in late afternoon, wilting by late morning the next day. The seeds are eaten by finches.

FLOWER TYPE **Regular** LEAF TYPE **Simple** LEAF ATTACHMENT **Alternate** FRUIT **Pod**

fruit

Buffalo Gourd
Cucurbita foetidissima

Family: Gourd (Cucurbitaceae)

Height: 5–20' (1.5–6.1 m); vine

Flower: broad, trumpet-shaped, orange or yellow flowers, 3½–5" (9–13 cm) long; petals flare widely into 5 pointed wrinkled lobes

Leaf: large, heart-shaped, grayish-green leaves, 6–12" (15–30 cm) long, have finely toothed edges, are white below, roughly textured, and foul smelling

Fruit: gourd-like, resembling a little round watermelon, 3" (7.5 cm) wide, smooth with green-and-white stripes, then turns all yellow when ripe; pumpkin-like seeds

Bloom: Jul–Sep

Cycle/Origin: perennial; native

Zone/Habitat: desert scrub, grasslands, oak/pinyon pine/juniper woods, montane at 1,000–7,000' (305–2,135 m); along roads and washes, disturbed areas, canyons

Range: northern half and southeastern quarter of Arizona

Notes: Also called coyote melon, it's closely related to garden pumpkins. Indigenous Peoples have used this plant for at least 9,000 years, extracting oil for cooking from the edible seeds, or roasting and salting them to eat. The Navajo have used the dried fruit to make gourd rattles used during ceremonies. The crushed leaves are an effective insecticide and the fetid-smelling (thus the species name, *foetidissima*) chemicals they contain are being studied for other possible uses.

FLOWER TYPE	LEAF TYPE	LEAF ATTACHMENT	FRUIT
Tube	**Simple**	**Alternate**	**Pod**

Scrambled Eggs

Corydalis aurea

Family: Poppy (Papaveraceae)

Height: 8–12" (20–30 cm)

Flower: irregularly shaped, tubular yellow flowers, ¾" (2 cm) long, attached horizontally in spike clusters, 3–4" (7.5–10 cm) long; each bloom has 4 fused petals; top petal forms a hood and a broad, hollow, downward-curving spur; bottom fringed petal is lip-like and drooping

Leaf: feathery, bluish-green leaves, 3–6" (7.5–15 cm) long, with pairs of lobed leaflets; reddish-green stems

Fruit: thin curved flattened seedpods, 1" (2.5 cm) long

Bloom: Feb–Jun

Cycle/Origin: annual, biennial; native

Zone/Habitat: desert scrub, grasslands, oak/pinyon pine/juniper woodlands and montane at 1,500–9,000' (460–2,745 m); disturbed areas, along washes, old fields

Range: throughout, except the southwestern corner

Notes: The Navajo have used this plant medicinally for various ailments and as a disinfectant. It contains toxic alkaloids. Each of the seeds has a nutritious blob attached that ants consume, but it contains chemicals that repel mice. The ants collect the seeds and store them belowground, where the seeds remain after the ants eat the blob. This protects the seeds from wildfires as well as mice, which are kept out of the ant colonies by the soldier ants.

CLUSTER TYPE	FLOWER TYPE	LEAF TYPE	LEAF ATTACHMENT	FRUIT
Spike	**Irregular**	**Compound**	**Alternate**	**Pod**

fruit

Melon Loco
Apodanthera undulata

Family: Gourd (Cucurbitaceae)

Height: 8–10' (2.4–3 m); vine

Flower: star-shaped yellow flowers, 3–5" (7.5–13 cm) wide, with 5 limp wavy oval petals fused at the bases around a light-yellow center; male flowers in loose clusters; larger female blooms are solitary

Leaf: kidney-shaped, dark-green leaves, 2–6" (5–15 cm) wide, rough, hairy with lobed or wavy ruffled edges

Fruit: oval or round, hairy hard-shelled melon, 2½–4" (6–10 cm) long, is dark green and turns light green when ripe; has dark ridges that run lengthwise

Bloom: Jun–Sep

Cycle/Origin: perennial; native

Zone/Habitat: desert scrub, grasslands, oak/pinyon pine/juniper woodlands at 1,500–5,500' (460–1,675 m); flats, along roads and washes, floodplains

Range: southeastern quarter of Arizona and the central part of the state

Notes: It can have both male and female flowers, but it only develops the female flowers after reaching a certain size. This coarse vine is well adapted to drought, with its large taproot and long, large side roots that absorb and store any surface water. Its roots are high in starch. The melon is bitter, but it has been eaten during famine. It ranges from Arizona east to Texas and south into northern Mexico.

FLOWER TYPE
Regular

LEAF TYPE
Simple

LEAF TYPE
Simple Lobed

LEAF ATTACHMENT
Alternate

FRUIT
Pod

Common Sunflower
Helianthus annuus

Family: Aster (Asteraceae)

Height: 3–10' (.9–3 m)

Flower: sunny-yellow flower head, 3–6" (7.5–15 cm) wide, with 15–20 yellow petals surrounding a large dark-brown or purple center; 2–20 flowers per plant

Leaf: broadly triangular or heart-shaped leaves, 3–12" (7.5–30 cm) long, stiff hairs, coarsely and irregularly toothed; leaves alternate along a very coarse stem

Bloom: Mar–Oct

Cycle/Origin: annual; native

Zone/Habitat: most life zones at 100–7,000' (305–2,135 m); fields, along roads, disturbed ground

Range: throughout

Notes: It's a smaller, wild version of giant sunflower, which is the large cultivated plant often grown in gardens and fields and from which seeds are harvested. Unlike the giant variety, common sunflower usually branches several times, but it is similar in that it produces many nutritious seeds. Used for food by many peoples historically, the seeds can be ground or pressed to make flour, oil, dyes—even medicine. It's often seen growing along highways, where the seeds of maturing plants are dispersed along the road by wind created from passing cars and trucks. Sunflowers do not follow the sun, as is widely believed. Flower heads face the morning sun once the plant matures and begins to bloom, thus most flowers face east.

FLOWER TYPE **Composite**   LEAF TYPE **Simple**   LEAF ATTACHMENT **Alternate**

leaf cluster

Smooth Goldenrod
Solidago missouriensis

Family: Aster (Asteraceae)

Height: 12–36" (30–91 cm)

Flower: golden-yellow clusters, 3–6" (7.5–15 cm) long, of many tiny, daisy-like flower heads, ¼" (0.6 cm) wide; each bloom has 5–14 petals (ray flowers) around a yellow center

Leaf: lance-shaped, shiny and smooth, dark-green leaves, 2–6" (5–15 cm) long, with smooth edges that curl upward; upper leaves are shorter and narrow; a few tiny leaves cluster in each leaf junction (axis); leaves alternate along the smooth reddish stem

Bloom: Jun–Aug

Cycle/Origin: perennial; native

Zone/Habitat: grasslands, oak/pinyon pine/juniper woods, montane at 5,000–9,000' (1,525–2,745 m); open forests

Range: throughout, except the southwestern corner

Notes: "Goldenrod" is an apt description for this upright narrow plant topped with bright-yellow flower clusters. It's one of nine species of *Solidago* in Arizona, but smooth goldenrod is distinguished by the tiny leaf clusters in each leaf axis (see inset). It grows in large clumps, sending up numerous branchless stems from spreading underground runners. Indigenous Peoples have chewed the roots to ease toothaches. Widespread in most of the West and Midwest, it decorates areas along highways and railroads in late summer.

CLUSTER TYPE	FLOWER TYPE	LEAF TYPE	LEAF ATTACHMENT
Spike	**Composite**	**Simple**	**Alternate**

Broom Ragwort
Senecio spartioides

Family: Aster (Asteraceae)

Height: ½–3½' (15–107 cm); shrub

Flower: flat-topped yellow clusters, 4–8" (10–20 cm) wide, of 10–20 daisy-like flower heads, 3/4" (2 cm) wide; each bloom has 4–8 slightly drooping, non-over-lapping, narrow yellow petals with double-notched tips, surrounding a small orange center

Leaf: narrow and long or thread-like, bright-green leaves, 2–4" (5–10 cm) long, are smooth with smooth edges; lower leaves die before flowers open

Bloom: Jul–Oct

Cycle/Origin: perennial; native

Zone/Habitat: grasslands, oak/pinyon pine/juniper woodlands, montane at 6,500–9,000' (1,980–2,745 m); open disturbed or sandy areas, along streams, canyons

Range: throughout

Notes: This airy, bright-green shrub has many multibranched stems with lots of yellow flower heads in wide flat clusters. The lower leaves wither and fall off by the time the plant blooms, making it appear dead below. It is abundant during late summer in northern Arizona, where it grows in rocky high-elevation grasslands, forming large colonies among the grasses. Threadleaf ragwort (pg. 349) is similar to broom ragwort, but it is hairy overall and has divided leaves.

CLUSTER TYPE	FLOWER TYPE	LEAF TYPE	LEAF ATTACHMENT
Flat	**Composite**	**Simple**	**Alternate**

Goldenpea
Thermopsis montana

Family: Pea or Bean (Fabaceae)

Height: 24–36" (61–91 cm)

Flower: dense spike cluster, 5–12" (13–30 cm) long, of large, pea-like, bright-yellow flowers, 1" (2.5 cm) long

Leaf: bright-green leaves, 8" (20 cm) long, divided into 3 oval leaflets, 4" (10 cm) long, with pointed tips, prominent central veins, smooth edges; pairs of small appendages (stipules) at bases of leafstalks

Fruit: straight, flattened bean-like pod, 3" (7.5 cm) long, is stalkless, erect, and fuzzy green, turning smooth and tan when mature

Bloom: Apr–Jul

Cycle/Origin: perennial; native

Zone/Habitat: montane and subalpine at 6,000–11,000' (1,830–3,355 m); in openings among coniferous trees, in moist soils

Range: northern half of Arizona

Notes: This conspicuous flower spreads by underground roots, sending up stems at closely spaced intervals and forming colonies of plants as tall as 2–3 feet (61–91 cm). The large, pea-like flowers are shaped like lupine blooms, thus the genus name *Thermopsis*, from the Greek thermos for "lupine" and opsis for "similar." The foliage is avoided by livestock, but it is required food for caterpillars of the large and showy Queen Alexandra sulphur butterfly.

CLUSTER TYPE	FLOWER TYPE	LEAF TYPE	LEAF ATTACHMENT	FRUIT
Spike	**Irregular**	**Compound**	**Alternate**	**Pod**

417

Fiddleneck
Amsinckia menziesii

Family: Forget-me-not (Boraginaceae)

Height: 8–20" (20–50 cm)

Flower: yellow-to-yellowish-orange flowers in a coiled spike cluster, 8" (20 cm) long; each trumpet-shaped flower is ⅙–½" (0.4–1 cm) long and has a reddish-orange throat; buds and stems are covered with fine white hairs

Leaf: basal leaves, 1–6" (2.5–15 cm) long, are narrowly lance-shaped, dark green, and stalkless; stem leaves are gradually shorter farther up the stem; prickly white hairs cover the stems and leaves

Fruit: greenish red pod, turning brown, ⅝–1" (1.5–2.5 cm) long, is bean-like, slender, and flattened

Bloom: Mar–May

Cycle/Origin: annual; native

Zone/Habitat: desert scrub, grasslands below 4,000' (1,220 m); disturbed areas, along washes and roads, flats

Range: throughout Arizona, except northeastern corner

Notes: The common name refers to the resemblance of the flower spike to the neck of a violin, which is also coiled at its end. The bright flowers open first at the top of the coil, which gradually straightens as the lower flowers open. Large fallow fields sometimes contain many fiddlenecks; grazing cows avoid eating the plants because they contain alkaloids that are poisonous to livestock.

CLUSTER TYPE
Spike

FLOWER TYPE
Tube

LEAF TYPE
Simple

LEAF ATTACHMENT
Alternate

LEAF ATTACHMENT
Basal

COMMON NONNATIVE AND/OR INVASIVE SPECIES IN ARIZONA

Because these plants are nonnative, we're not covering them in detail here. Nonetheless, because some are invasive or have a tendency to spread aggressively, it's important to be aware of them. Here are some nonnative species:

Alfalfa
Medicago sativa

Common Dandelion
Taraxacum officinale

Common Mullein
Verbascum thapsus

Field Bindweed
Convolvulus arvensis

Filaree
Erodium cicutarium

Ivyleaf Morning Glory
Ipomoea hederacea

Shepherd's Purse
Capsella bursa-pastoris

Spiny Sow-thistle
Sonchus asper

Spreading Fanpetals
Sida abulifolia

Tall Morning Glory
Ipomoea purpurea

Yellow Sweet Clover
Melilotus officinalis

GLOSSARY

Alternate: A type of leaf attachment in which the leaves are singly and alternately attached along a stem, not paired or in whorls.

Annual: A plant that germinates, flowers, and sets seed during a single growing season and returns the following year from seed only.

Anther: A part of the male flower that contains the pollen.

Arroyo: A usually dry and sandy streambed in the Southwest over which water flows during or after heavy rains. See wash.

Axis: A point on the main stem from which lateral branches arise.

Basal: The leaves at the base of a plant near the ground, usually grouped in a round rosette.

Bell flower: A single, downward-hanging flower that has petals fused together, forming a bell-like shape. See tube flower.

Berry: A fleshy fruit that contains one or many seeds.

Biennial: A plant that lives for two years, blooming in the second year.

Bract: A leaf-like structure usually found at the base of a flower, often appearing as a petal.

Bulb: A short, round, underground shoot that is used as a food storage system, common in the Lily family.

Calyx: A collective group of all of the sepals of a flower.

Capsule: A pod-like fruiting structure that contains many seeds and has more than one chamber. See pod.

Cauline: The leaves that attach to the stem distinctly above the ground, as opposed to basal leaves, which attach near the ground.

Clasping: A type of leaf attachment in which the leaf base partly surrounds the main stem of the plant at the point of attachment; grasping the stem without a leafstalk.

Cluster: A group or collection of flowers or leaves.

Composite flower: A collection of tiny or small flowers that appears as one large flower, usually made up of ray and disk flowers, common in the Aster family.

Compound leaf: A single leaf that is composed of a central stalk and two or more leaflets.

Corolla: All of the petals of a flower that fuse together to form a tube.

Creosote bush: A yellow-flowered evergreen bush with a resinous odor, most strongly fragrant after rainfall, abundant in Southwest deserts.

Disk flower: One of many small, tubular flowers in the central part (disk) of a composite flower, common in the Aster family.

Ephemeral: Lasting for only a short time each spring.

Flat cluster: A group of flowers that forms a flat-topped structure, which allows flying insects to easily land and complete pollination.

Gland: A tiny structure that usually secretes oil or nectar, sometimes found on leaves, stems, stalks, and flowers, as in curlycup gumweed.

Globular: Having a spherical or globe-like shape.

Indigenous: Originating naturally in a particular region or environment.

Irregular flower: A flower that does not have the typical round shape, usually made up of five or more petals that are fused together in an irregular shape, common in the Pea or Bean family.

Keel: The two lower petals, often fused together, of a flower in the Pea or Bean family.

Leaflet: One of two or more leaf-like parts of a compound leaf.

Lip: The projection of a flower petal or the "odd" petal, such as the large inflated petal common in the Snapdragon family; sometimes, the lobes of a petal. See lobe.

Lobe: A large rounded projection of a petal or leaf, larger than the tooth of a leaf.

Lobed leaf: A simple leaf with at least one indentation (sinus) along an edge that does not reach the center or base of the leaf, as in common dandelion.

Margin: The edge of a leaf.

Mesa: An elevated, flat expanse of land (plateau), with one or more steep sides or cliffs; Spanish for "tableland."

Node: The place or point of origin on a stem where leaves attach or have been attached.

Nutlet: A small or diminutive nut or seed.

Opposite: A type of leaf attachment in which the leaves are situated directly across from each other on a stem.

Palmate leaf: A type of compound leaf in which three or more leaflets arise from a common central point at the end of a leafstalk, as in arroyo lupine.

Parasitic: A plant or fungus that derives its food or water chiefly from another plant, to the detriment of the host plant. See semiparasitic.

Perennial: A plant that lives from several to many seasons, returning each year from its roots.

Perfoliate: A type of leaf attachment in which the bases of at least two leaves connect around the main stem so that the stem appears to pass through one stalkless leaf.

Petal: A basic flower part that is usually brightly colored, serving to attract pollinating insects.

Photosynthesis: In green plants, the conversion of water and carbon dioxide into carbohydrates (food) from the energy in sunlight.

Pistil: The female part of a flower made up of an ovary, style, and stigma, often in the center of the flower.

Playa: The flat bottom of a desert valley, temporarily covered with water after heavy rains.

Pod: A dry fruiting structure that contains many seeds, often with a single chamber. See capsule.

Pollination: The transfer of pollen from the male anther to the female stigma, usually resulting in the production of seeds.

Radial spine: One of the outermost spines of a cluster, radiating from the longer central spines, spreading and pressed flat against the stem, as in cacti.

Ray flower: One of many individual outer flowers of a composite flower, common in the Aster family.

Recurved: Curved backward or downward, as in bracts or sepals.

Regular flower: A flower with 3 to 20 typical petals that are arranged in a circle.

Rhizome: A creeping, (usually) horizontal, underground stem.

Rosette: A cluster of leaves arranged in a circle, often at the base of the plant, as in common mullein.

Round cluster: A group of many flowers that forms a round structure, giving the appearance of one large flower.

Seed head: A group or cluster of seeds

Semiparasitic: A type of plant or fungus that derives a portion, but not all, of its food or water chiefly from another plant, to the detriment of the host plant. See parasitic.

Sepal: A member of the outermost set of petals of a flower, typically green or leafy, but often colored and resembling a petal.

Simple leaf: A single leaf with an undivided or unlobed edge.

Spike cluster: A group of many flowers on a single, spike-like stem, giving the appearance of one large flower.

Spine: A modified leaf; a stiff, usually short, sharply pointed outgrowth. See thorn.

Spur: A hollow, tube-like appendage of a flower, usually where nectar is located, as in golden columbine.

Stamen: The male parts of a flower, consisting of a filament and an anther.

Standard: The uppermost petal of a flower in the Pea or Bean family.

Stem leaf: Any leaf that grows along the stem of a plant, as opposed to a leaf at the base of a plant. See cauline and basal.

Stigma: The female part of the flower that receives the pollen.

Stipule: A basal appendage (usually in pairs) of a leaf that is not attached to the leaf blade, as in goldenpea.

Taproot: The primary, vertically descending root of a plant.

Tendril: A twining, string like structure of a vine that clings to plants or other objects for support.

Terminal: Growing at the end of a leaf, stem, or stalk

Thorn: A modified part of a stem; a stiff, usually long, and sharply pointed outgrowth. See spine.

Throat: The opening or orifice of a tubular flower (corolla or calyx).

Toothed: Having a jagged or serrated edge of a leaf, resembling teeth of a saw.

Tube flower: A flower with fused petals forming a tube and usually turned upward. See bell flower.

Umbel: A domed to relatively flat-topped flower cluster that resembles the overall shape of an open umbrella, common in the Carrot family.

Wash: A usually dry-and-sandy streambed in the Southwest over which water flows during or after heavy rains. See arroyo.

Whorled: A type of attachment in which a circle or ring of three or more similar leaves, stems, or flowers originate from a common point.

Wing: A flat extension at the base of a leaf or edge of a leafstalk, sometimes extending down the stem of the plant; one of the side petals of a flower, common in the Pea or Bean family.

Woody: Having the appearance or texture resembling wood, as in stems, bark, or taproots.

CHECKLIST/INDEX BY SPECIES

Use the boxes to check the flowers you've seen.

427

ABOUT THE AUTHORS

Nora Mays Bowers

Nora Mays Bowers is a writer and nature photographer. She likes being outdoors—looking at birds, wildlife, and plants. Long ago, she earned a Master of Science degree in Ecology from the University of Arizona. She is the primary author of *Wildflowers of Arizona, Wildflowers of the Carolinas, Wildflowers of Texas, Cactus of Texas, Cactus of the Southwest,* and *Kaufman Focus Guides: Mammals of North America.* Most of the photographs in these guides were taken by her and her husband, Rick.

Rick Bowers

Rick Bowers began birding at age 10 while living on Ft. Huachuca, Arizona. In less than a year he was leading birders to the specialty birds of southeastern Arizona, and he continued to lead tours during high school and college. After college, Rick led bird-watching tours for Victor Emanuel Nature Tours for 16 years. Now, when not working on books or photography, Rick leads photography and birding tours around the world through his company, Bowers Birding & Photo Safaris.

Stan Tekiela

Naturalist, wildlife photographer, and writer Stan Tekiela is the originator of the popular state-specific field guide series that includes *Birds of Arizona Field Guide.* Stan has authored more than 190 educational books, including field guides, quick guides, nature books, children's books, playing cards, and more, presenting many species of animals and plants. With a Bachelor of Science degree in Natural History from the University of Minnesota and as an active professional naturalist for more than 30 years, Stan studies and photographs wildlife throughout the United States and Canada. He has received various national and regional awards for his books and photographs. Also a well-known columnist and radio personality, his syndicated column appears in more than 25 newspapers, and his wildlife programs are broadcast on a number of Midwest radio stations. Stan can be contacted via his website, naturesmart.com.

The Story of AdventureKEEN

We are an independent nature and outdoor activity publisher. Our founding dates back more than 40 years, guided then and now by our love of being in the woods and on the water, by our passion for reading and books, and by the sense of wonder and discovery made possible by spending time recreating outdoors in beautiful places.

It is our mission to share that wonder and fun with our readers, especially with those who haven't yet experienced all the physical and mental health benefits that nature and outdoor activity can bring.

#bewellbeoutdoors